MANNERHOUSE

A Play in a Prologue and Three Acts

Books by

THOMAS WOLFE

Look Homeward, Angel

Of Time and the River

From Death to Morning

The Story of a Novel

The Face of a Nation

A Stone, a Leaf, a Door

Thomas Wolfe's Letters to His Mother

Gentlemen of the Press

The Web and the Rock

You Can't Go Home Again

The Hills Beyond

Mannerhouse

MANNERHOUSE

A Play

in a Prologue and Three Acts

by

Thomas Wolfe

NEW YORK

HARPER & BROTHERS PUBLISHERS

1948

11-8

FIRST EDITION

K-X

MANNERHOUSE

A Play in a Prologue and Three Acts

PERSONS IN THE PROLOGUE

RAMSAY
THE MINISTER
MULATTO
SAVAGE CHIEFTAIN
ROBERT, Ramsay's son
Negro slaves

PERSONS IN THE PLAY

GENERAL RAMSAY
MRS. RAMSAY
EUGENE RAMSAY ⎱ their sons
RALPH RAMSAY ⎰
MAJOR PATTON
MARGARET, his daughter
CADET
MR. PORTER
TOD, old Negro servant
BYNUM, a young Negro
FIRST CARPENTER
SECOND CARPENTER
Guests at General Ramsay's home, Mannerhouse
Slaves and servants
Soldiers

Time of the Prologue: Colonial Period
Time of the Play: First Act: 1861
                           Second Act: 1865
                           Third Act: A few years later

Prologue

SCENE: *Upon a hillside in the South two hundred years ago.*
A primitive landscape is in the process of conversion.
Here, on top, where the hill is round, and before it
slopes away to the East, a clearing has been made in
the dense undergrowth of young pine, oak, chestnut,
and laurel. It is early summer, but in that warm lush
wooded place, the brown and fragrant needles of the
pines yet carpet the earth.
In the foreground are the stumps of trees white and
bleeding fresh. In the background, black barred
against a red and smoky sun which is sloping swiftly
into the west, is a forest of great pines.
Beside the pines, upon the very brink of the hill,
before it drops, a house is rearing its white and comely
sides. From within comes the sound of hammering,
and the shearing of boards, and a low steady sustained
and savage chant sung by deep barbaric voices.
To the left, a wide path has been cut straight
down the flank of the hill through the dense growth:
in that green place it bleeds like a wound.
From below there are cries and confused noises, and
the sound of men crashing through the thickets.
Near the path, and slant-wise across the clearing, a

great white column of the house lies at its length upon the ground.

Behind the column, and above the entrance to the path, a man is standing on guard. His attitude is at once casual and alert; he bears loosely but handily in the crook of his arm a long barreled rifle, and when he moves his long brown sinewy figure even slightly, he is alive with the slow yet rapid stealth of a cat.

He wears a shirt of a coarse white stuff, open at his corded neck; his clothes are of a rough spun substance, brown.

His face is the face of a gentleman who has gone out to subdue a kingdom for himself; its gentleness and sweetness has been replaced by sternness, inflexibility, resolve. The forehead is high and narrow; the head is a small lean box, carried fiercely and swiftly and beautifully above his straight body; the eyes are sunken well below thick brows; mouth and nose are straight and thin; and there is upon the man very little flesh; there is nothing which is not carried gauntly and magnificently.

Before this man, up and down the path, into the house and back again, bearing in upon their bodies heavy baskets holding bricks, or beams, or pieces of timber, coming out with bodies bent by labor, huge, sinister, gorillalike, is passing and repassing an endless chain of savage black men. They are naked save for short trousers which extend to the knee; their great bodies gleam with sweat; their faces are contorted by the shrill brute agony of their labors. For the most part they are silent, although occasionally they jabber a few words to one another in an outlandish tongue.

Their leader, evidently, is a huge man, stronger, fiercer, more savage looking than the rest, but with the pride of majesty upon him. He bears the heaviest loads—he bears them with fierce contemptuous ease —and occasionally he shouts and snarls at them in tones of heavy command.

A small Negro, a MULATTO, *a little man with a sharp, furtive, weazened face, and apparently an overseer, for he wears shoes and a hat, walks back and forth, eyeing the men and occasionally directing them about the disposition of the heaviest pieces of timber.*

And the white man never ceases to watch them with his quick, fierce eyes.

There is a stirring in the path; a little man in ministerial garb, with the bones and quick movements of a bird, and with the agony of salvation on his pinched small face, comes up, clasping the Gospels in his hand.

There is a wind in the tall pines.

MINISTER
To the man on guard
You are Mr. Ramsay?

RAMSAY

Looking but not moving

That is my name, sir.

MINISTER

I am the minister in the village.

A pause

RAMSAY

Inflexibly

Yes. There is a village, I suppose.

MINISTER

Doubtfully

I have come to bid you welcome.

RAMSAY

Coldly, a little fiercely

Thank you, sir.

MINISTER

I am glad to know you, sir.

He extends his hand. RAMSAY *takes it briefly, crushes it, and discards it.*

MINISTER

You are not alone, I believe. That was your son, perhaps, that I saw directing the workmen at the foot of the hill.

RAMSAY

That is my son Robert.

MINISTER

And the rest of your family—where are they?

PROLOGUE

RAMSAY

My wife and the girls will come from Virginia—when my house is built.

MINISTER

We shall be glad to welcome them when they come. You will find us a friendly and neighborly folk—a God-fearing folk.

RAMSAY

Thank you. My wife enjoys neighbors: she likes to go to church.

A pause

MINISTER

And you as well, I hope, sir.

A pause

RAMSAY

Coldly, implacably

I must build my house.

MINISTER

Awkwardly

It is a beautiful and enduring structure.

RAMSAY

In a low, fierce, exultant voice which rises toward the end

My house will be more strong than death; it will possess and make its own the lives of valiant men and women when I and my sons are gone. I have built it here on this high hill, where it may catch the sun at night and dawn, when all the world is dark. And on this column of my house you will find our motto engraved in bronze.

The MINISTER *approaches and reads.*

MINISTER

Nil Separabit.

RAMSAY

"Nothing shall part us"—not while the house may stand and take us in its arms to give us rest and shelter. So may it comfort me. So, I pray God, may it comfort my son and his sons. I say, God keep such houses, and all who rest in them!

MINISTER

Amen, amen—Your house is like a live thing to you.

RAMSAY

Some houses are like people—if you should cut them they would bleed.

MINISTER

My Father's House is like that, Mr. Ramsay. Ah, you should be thankful to the goodness of Him who has so blessed you.

RAMSAY

A little ironically

Yes?

MINISTER

For He has given you wealth, a fine family; and finally He has shown His trust in you by delivering these heathen into your keeping.

PROLOGUE

Ah, but that is friendly of Him, isn't it?

With genuine pride in his voice

But they are a likely set, aren't they? I got them, by the way, in the Fort of Charleston in South Carolina, from one of the Lord's servants.

MINISTER

Oh—a missionary.

RAMSAY

No, a ship's captain from Salem in Massachusetts.

The MINISTER turns and begins to harangue the passing blacks. They understand from his tone and manner that he is addressing them, and they stare curiously at the tight-faced little man who thus harangues them.

MINISTER

"Servants, be obedient to thy masters, not only to the good and gentle, but also to the forward." Ephesians 6:5. "Thou shalt seek for bondmen of the heathen that are round about ye: of them shall ye have bondmen and bondmaids." Leviticus 25:44.

The blacks turn to each other with broad grins, and jabber in their strange tongue, gesticulating and pointing toward him.

He shows some irritation at their conduct, but continues, growing more and more solemn as he goes on.

"The faithful servant shall be given peaceful labors; I shall wither the wicked in my wrath." Proverbs 10:7.

[7]

*By this time, the blacks, tickled at his rapid gesticula-
tions, and his earnest, vehement tones, are chuckling
and laughing openly. Somewhat enraged at their conduct, and not understanding the reason, he continues
with great bitterness.*

Aye, laugh if ye will, in your heathenish fashion, but I draw
my warrant from the scriptures of the Old and New Testa-
ment—the sole, the only revealed word of God. So, hear
ye and take warning. "He that knoweth his master's will
and doeth it not, shall be beaten with many stripes." Luke
XII, 47.

RAMSAY

Quietly, with irony
I am afraid they don't understand you.

MINISTER

Incredulously
Don't understand me!

RAMSAY

Not a word, I'm afraid. You see, God has neglected to teach
them English. If you could only say to them then, what you
have just said—
He makes an expressive gesture of his hands.
It would do a great deal of good, I am sure. They are savage
and ignorant, and stand in need of your teaching.

MINISTER

In an ecstasy
No, now, now. Did not Christ's disciples go out among the
highways and byways of the world converting strange

peoples? I should be unworthy of my cloth if I refused to do the same now.

Yes, Minister. And so?

And so, let us invoke God's mercy for the salvation of these souls which have lived so long in darkness. Let us pray.

With the same strange irony
Thy will be done. Shall they kneel?

That would be best.

> RAMSAY *stops his men with a single gesture, and by motions indicates that he desires them to kneel. They do not understand. Finally, he goes to each in turn, forces him down upon his knees and raises his arms in an attitude of supplication. All obey, except the giant black who alone seems to have grasped the significance of the business. He backs away angrily and rebelliously, talking fiercely and peremptorily to his subjects, commanding them to rise. Some get up, others look doubtfully from the white man to the black. The question is now much more important than that of religious conversion: it is a question of obedience and supremacy.* RAMSAY *sternly motions the rebel to assume a kneeling posture. He refuses, withdrawing fiercely and proudly; the white man*

settles the matter by approaching the rebel and knocking him to the ground with a blow of his fist. All then kneel. RAMSAY *returns and takes up his old watchful position slightly behind the* MINISTER.

RAMSAY

Grimly, coldly, quietly

I think you may begin now.

MINISTER

The MINISTER *bows his head and prays.*

Almighty God, our gracious Heavenly Father, we come to Thee today on bended knees, invoking Thy tender love and guidance, and asking of Thee, like Solomon, no greater boon than wisdom. Oh God, we beseech Thee, be merciful to us, and to those with us, and to those about us, and to these wretched heathen whom Thou hast delivered unto our care; vouchsafe that we may be kind and just and temperate in our dealings with them, and that we may lead them with Thy love, from the dark forest. Thou hast made men, O God—likewise hast Thou made masters—Thou has put Thy mark and Thy injunction on both. Some, in time past, O God, were good and dutiful servants, and Thou blessed them, but the wicked and rebellious made a tower 'gainst Thee, and Thou smote them hip and thigh, and burnst their skins black, and put a mark whereby all men might know them, so that they were afraid before Thy wrath, and fled away into the strange, unknown places. And these Thou hast delivered unto us. Hear us and answer us, O God, so

that in time these souls which have lived in error may be brought to light, that through Christ's love and blood and sacrifice upon the Cross, the souls of these savages may all at length be saved. Now let us say the Lord's prayer:
Our Father which art in heaven
Hallowed be thy name,
Thy kingdom come,
Thy will be done,
On earth as it is in heaven.
Give us this day
Our daily bread
And forgive us our trespasses
As we forgive those
Who trespass against us.
And lead us not into Temptation,
But deliver us from evil,
For Thine is the Kingdom,
And the power and the glory
Forever and ever,
Amen.

> *The* MINISTER *is joined in the last part of the prayer by* RAMSAY. *When they are done, they pause and are silent for a moment in the quiet hush of the evening. During all this time, the blacks, holding their arms stiffly and solemnly erect, have listened with growing awe and wonder to the great cadences of the voices and the prayer. They have been very deeply stirred by the solemn rhythm of the man—by his fierce*

intensity. Now, at a sign from RAMSAY, *they rise again, and go about their work with a sort of wonder, passing and repassing silently into the house, listening dumbly to the low, fierce, bitter harangue of their fallen chief. The* MINISTER'S *face is alight with happiness, ecstasy.*

MINISTER

God will find a way! He will! He will! Did you see those black faces shine?

RAMSAY

Quietly

Yes, I think they were very much impressed.

MINISTER

God has found a way! Already his light has entered unto them—the light of our God, the true God, the Christian God!

RAMSAY

It was a very fine prayer, sir. You must come again.

MINISTER

Ah, friend, my work is just begun. I shall not rest until the idols are all overthrown.

RAMSAY

Then we shall see you soon.

MINISTER

I shall come daily until my work is done.

RAMSAY

Then, for the present, good-by, my friend.

PROLOGUE

God bless you, friend.

*They clasp hands, warmly this time, and the little
man reels off into the path as if drunken. And as he
goes, he sings with all the passion of his heart, a great
hymn about the Passion and the Blood of Christ. The
Negroes, never halting in their even stride, follow
him with many glances of the eye as he goes, giving
him a wide and respectful leeway.*

RAMSAY

*A straight, gray figure in the shadows as before, but
with a baffled look in his eyes—in a low voice*

If it were true! If it were true!

The Negroes resume their great low chant.

*It grows darker. The sun has set. Twilight. Dusk
comes quickly and the great black beasts go padding
in and out more swiftly.*

RAMSAY *stands again, a gray, swift, silent figure, in
the shadows back of the column. There is a stirring
in the bush behind him. He gives no sign that he has
heard. The great* SAVAGE CHIEFTAIN *comes from darkness like a cat and stands behind the white man, poised
upon his toes. In a moment he raises his huge right
arm and brandishes lightly there a short-handled,
brightly gleaming ax. The little* MULATTO, *stationed
just in front of his master, has seen the whole occur-
rence. With eyes that are glazed with horror, he
squeaks twice like a frightened rat, and the white*

[13]

man hurls himself downward to the earth, as the ax whirls over and above him, and sinks itself, quivering, in the wood of the column. The SAVAGE *springs like a cat upon the prostrate body of his master, but is knocked senseless by a blow from* RAMSAY'S *gun stock. The white man leaps to his feet and confronts the threatening blacks who have rushed to the spot and stand in a baleful circle. With his rifle, he forces them back into the path, and along their processional, holding them at bay, while he dispatches the* MULATTO *for his son.*

RAMSAY

Curtly

Go tell my son Robert to come here.

The MULATTO *runs off into the path and returns presently with the son—a slender, fair-skinned, blond young man of twenty-three or -four years. He also is armed.*

Sharply

Go behind me, Robert.

ROBERT

Trembling

What is it?

RAMSAY

The big one tried to kill me with an ax. Now we must watch them. They are ugly.

ROBERT *shudders but takes up his position behind his father.*

Turn your back to me so that you'll be facing the other way.

> ROBERT *does so.*

Now we're ready for whatever happens!

> *The* SAVAGE CHIEFTAIN *on the ground moves.*

ROBERT

> *Hoarsely*

Father!

RAMSAY

Yes?

ROBERT

He's not dead! He moved!

RAMSAY

> *Grimly*

It is well. He was strong before; now he will be faithful.

> *The great black body begins to drag itself slowly and painfully toward the path.*

ROBERT

Father! He's going!

RAMSAY

Let him go! I have put my mark upon him!

> *Suddenly the great black gets to his feet, turns suddenly, and advances toward the white man.*
>
> RAMSAY *makes a threatening movement with his rifle. With a gesture in which there is majesty and dignity, without any servility, the* SAVAGE *falls to his knees and acknowledges obedience to his new king by kiss-*

ing his hand. Then he arises, lurches drunkenly into the path, and disappears.

RAMSAY

In a low tone filled with terrible satisfaction

It is the first time a king has kissed my hand. What he has done the others must do. I will be king in my own right.

The great black figures, bearing in their heavy burdens, coming out with bodies bent, huge, sinister, gorillalike, pad swiftly and softly past. And ever as they go, the white man watches them warily and warns them back into their trodden path, and turns lightly on his feet in a half-circle, so that always he is facing them, in the manner of a circus man in a cage with animals. And as they go now in the dark, faster and faster as it seems, a mad barbaric chant comes low and fierce from their deep throats. Silence and darkness. The even sustained noises of little night things—crickets and whippoorwills. The little MULATTO *no longer trusts himself away from the feet of his master: he crouches, tense, stricken, moaning softly to himself.*

In a low, still voice, at length

My God! Is this, then, how a prayer is answered?

With a cry

Oh then, our cause is one, God.

A wind blows through the pines. All the million-noted little creatures of the night have come to life and are singing now in a vast, low chorus: a weird

[16]

ululation which seems to continue and prolong the deep chant of the savages; which seems to hold in it the myriad voices of their demons. The young man shudders convulsively and slips down weakly until he sits upon the column, his rifle at rest beside him. RAMSAY *continues to stand gauntly above the figures of the* MULATTO *and his son. His face is at once stern, slightly contemptuous, yet strangely tender. The pines are bent by the wind again.*

The great black figures continue to pad swiftly and softly past. A church bell rings slowly and sweetly, far away.

Curtain

Act One

SCENE: *When the curtain rises, all within the house is dark,*
though on the porch outside between the contour
of the great white columns, the moon has printed
blocks of misty radiance.

Outside may be heard the noises of the encampment
—the shouts and cries of men, the shrill whinnying
of horses, the coming and going of feet, confused,
disordered, as they would actually.

Blended, but coming from the house, is the sound of
music, slow, soft, seductive—the feet of dancers, and
the voices of many people, men and women, boys
and girls—fine, young, melodious.

Bugles are sounded, for it is Spring, 1861.

There is a wind about the corners of the house; a
thin grey spume of clouds is washed about the
window of the moon; the scene is darkened.

All the sounds become ordered; the noise of the en-
campment sinks into a steady, distant hum with
momentary climaxes.

Within the house, the lights blaze on. The scene is
GENERAL RAMSAY'S *study. To the right, there are*
windows and French windows through which the
white columns of the front porch are seen. From the

door in the back wall, leading to the hall, BYNUM, *a very black young Negro, and three more Negro servants carry glasses, champagne bottles and buckets with ice, crossing the room to the door at the left which connects the study with other rooms of the mansion. There the farewell party takes place.* TOD, *a giant Negro, a man of terrible and savage majesty, which even the coat and buttons of the butler cannot conceal, directs the four menservants with his eyes and occasional gestures.*

It is possible to detect, in the orderly confusion of young laughter and speech, certain recognizable phrases, originating in the adjoining quarters. They are saying.

All speaking at once

MAJOR'S VOICE

One hundred and nineteen of them, sir, and all under seventeen. They stepped forward to a man.

MARGARET'S VOICE

Where is Eugene?

Laughter

A YOUNG MAN'S VOICE

He's drunk.

Laughter

A WOMAN'S DARK VOICE

Feel for his family . . .

ACT ONE

A DEEP MAN'S VOICE

Outrageous . . . no manners . . .

A YOUNG GIRL'S VOICE

Ralph is handsome in his uniform.

A DEEP MAN'S VOICE

Shop-keeping Yankees.
The music has stopped.

A YOUNG GIRL'S VOICE

Isn't it thrilling! . . .

MAJOR'S VOICE

Six weeks, sir—drive the whole pack into Washington . . .

MANY VOICES TOGETHER

Music—music—where's the music.

MAJOR'S VOICE

Yes, I say six weeks, sir—no more.

A DEEP MAN'S VOICE

Snap your fingers at them, and they'll run like rabbits.
All laughing delightedly

MANY VOICES, old and young

Yes, yes. If you snap your fingers at them—
A great snapping of fingers is heard within the house.

A THIN HIGH VOICE

*Far and dim—in the upper air, but howling faintly
with malevolent laughter*

Snap your fingers, gentlemen. Snap your fingers.

[21]

SEVERAL GUESTS

In hushed voices

Who was that? Who was it?

Eugene—Always up to something, drunk as a lord, you know.

Laughter

Yes—yes—it was Eugene.

The moon drives out of heavy clouds, and the scene goes dimly visible again.

A VOICE

Speaking from the borders of the house

General!

GENERAL'S VOICE

Deep, calm, melodious

Yes?

VOICE

We are ready.

GENERAL'S VOICE

At midnight, then.

VOICE

Yes, sir.

The GENERAL, a man near sixty, with a thick, blunt beard, and a fine bold valiant face, crosses the room from the door at the right. TOD bows sternly, inflexibly, and opens the door at the left, leading to the quarter of the house where the dance goes on.

[22]

ACT ONE

Where is the music?

A waltz is played.

There is but one night in all the world, and it is yours. So dance, my boys and girls. Dance.

The music swells in volume until it sings to fill the house. Shadows of dancers are printed on the walls. MAJOR PATTON enters. He is a short man of apoplectic appearance—fine thick white hair above a red round face; loyal, prejudiced, courageous and intolerant. He speaks in a high fat thick wheezing voice, and seems forever panting out important news just gained.

MAJOR

And have you heard, sir? Have you heard? One hundred and seventeen of the men, all under nineteen, stepped forward. It was magnificent. The entire cadet corps.

GENERAL

You told me this morning.

TOD *goes out.*

MAJOR

In disbelief

Not really. But such spirit as that is unconquerable. With boys like these, we shall drive the shop-keeping Yankees back into Washington, pell-mell . . . in a month! In two weeks, General.

GENERAL

That is very wild and foolish talk.

[23]

MAJOR

Oh, come! You do not think this business will last any longer.

GENERAL

This business will last much longer. This business will eventuate as a very dangerous war!

MAJOR

Oh, nonsense, sir. A holiday only, pleasant exercise for our horses—call it what you will. But not a war, General.

GENERAL

A very desperate and determined war.

MAJOR

Then let us say two months or, say by autumn. I tell you it will be done by autumn. Three months—three months at the longest.

GENERAL

Three months! The winter, too, and longer.

MAJOR

Stammering slightly
But—but—see here—you know, against gentlemen—

GENERAL

Perhaps we shall be burdened by our armor. And the battle of Crécy was decided long ago.

MAJOR

In a low, but very earnest tone
Sir, I believe in gentlemen. It is my religion.

ACT ONE

GENERAL

I have said prayers, too, Major.

MAJOR

And I believe in justice and truth and honor—in our cause.

GENERAL

Our hearts are blind upon their warmest side, I think.

MAJOR

We must fight.

GENERAL

That is assured.

EUGENE passes outside under the window.

MAJOR

About Eugene—

GENERAL

Rising, a trifle brusquely

Yes?

MAJOR

It is most distressing. Known him as a boy, one of my cadets. I want to talk with you.

Music, which has stopped after the waltz, is played again.

GENERAL

Shall we return to the dancers?

They go out.

EUGENE, *a young man with a thin, bright face, a lad with dark intelligence, with lank black hair, and un-*

[25]

*kempt person, enters swiftly from the darkness be-
yond the windows. He crosses the room and pours
whisky from a decanter on the table. He drinks.*

*There is a sound of ribald laughter, and of maudlin
singing from the encampment outside.* EUGENE *goes
to the window, drunken voices salute him.*

THE MAUDLIN VOICES

Mockingly

Captain. Oh-oh! Captain!

EUGENE

With a gesture of his arm

Hi, boys!

VOICES

Loud with laughter

Our Captain's drunk!

EUGENE

Laughing unsteadily

Never mind that! What I say is: "What's the matter with
my manner, eh?"

Rapidly with a fierce cry

What's the matter with my manner?

*He is answered by a burst of ribald laughter, catcalls,
and mockery which subside presently. He comes to
the center of the room and stands perfectly motion-
less for a moment. His lean dark face writhes.*

TOD, *the giant Negro, appears with the swift stealth of
a great cat.*

ACT ONE

EUGENE

Sharply, without glancing round

Yes, Tod!

TOD

With a stern, grave bow

De Mist-ess want to see yo' sah.

EUGENE

Harshly

Say it without bowing, you old fool.

TOD

Bowing

Yes, sah.

EUGENE

Ironically, with a bow

I forgot: Your majesty!

TOD

Inflexibly

Yes, sah.

EUGENE

And so you have learned the manner, too? And your fathers were kings!

TOD

Yes, sah.

EUGENE

Old man, you have degenerated. You have become a gentleman. Kings do not have manners.

[27]

TOD

With the same stern courtliness

Yes, sah. The Mist-ess—

EUGENE

I will find her.

> TOD *bows and retires.* EUGENE *drinks again. A young* CADET, *a boy with straw-colored hair, enters the room.*

What's your name, boy?

CADET

Cameron, sir.

EUGENE

That's your last. And your first?

CADET

Dinwiddie.

EUGENE

Virginia, eh?

> CADET *nods.*

Where all good things come from?

> CADET *laughs.*

And most of the gentlemen.

> CADET *is silent.* EUGENE *drinks and is silent also for a moment. He puts down his glass. Presently*

Going to war, Cadet?

CADET

Yes, sir.

ACT ONE

EUGENE

Want to go?

CADET

With enthusiasm

Oh, yes, sir.

EUGENE

With cynical imitation

Oh, yes, sir. It will be great fun, won't it?

CADET

Eagerly

Oh, yes, sir.

EUGENE

Yes—great fun, Cadet, getting shot at in a pretty uniform with shiny buttons, so they can see you better.

He laughs.

He laughs again as he has laughed before—with a terrible note in his laughter.

Great fun, Cadet.

They are both silent.

Young, aren't you?

CADET

Hotly

I'm as old as the others—and bigger than most of them.

EUGENE

You wanted to go?

CADET

Fiercely

I've as much right to go as the others.

EUGENE

Yes, I suppose so. The supply of damned young fools is inexhaustible.

The CADET *turns stiffly on his heels.*

In more kindly tone

Come back, Cameron. I didn't mean to offend you. After all, you did the only thing you could do, didn't you?

CADET

Yes, sir. All the others volunteered.

EUGENE

And so did you?

CADET

Yes, sir.

EUGENE

Now tell me, Cadet—is there any particular branch of the service you would prefer?

CADET

Promptly

Yes, sir.

EUGENE

What is it?

CADET

The cavalry.

EUGENE

Oh, the cavalry! Like horses, eh?

[30]

CADET

Yes, sir.

EUGENE

The kind with lots of fire, you know. They step around like this.

> *He teeters about drunkenly on his legs, and they both laugh.*

CADET

Oh, yes. I like that kind.

> *A pause*

I like the uniform, too.

EUGENE

Oh, yes, the uniform. Spurs, eh?

CADET

Yes, sir. And a sash of yellow silk around the waist.

EUGENE

Oho! That's quite fine, isn't it?

CADET

Yes, sir. I like the hat, too.

EUGENE

Ah, the hat. And why the hat, cadet?

CADET

There is a plume—

EUGENE

> *With mockery that escapes unnoticed*

A plume! A plume! Just like those worn by the invincible knights of old.

CADET

With entire innocence

Yes, sir. But it doesn't stick straight up as theirs did. It goes around the side.

EUGENE

Why this is better and better. Cavalier fashion, eh?

CADET

Yes, sir.

EUGENE

And, no doubt, a sword that will clank, Cadet.

CADET

Yes, sir.

A slight pause

I have a picture of it here. Would you like to see it, sir?

EUGENE

By all means.

The CADET *fumbles at the pocket of his jacket, with trembling fingers and draws forth a small object wrapped carefully in tissue paper, tied with a ribbon of silk.*

Ah, precious!

CADET

Removing the paper

You see, sir.

EUGENE

Examining the picture

Ah, yes, a very handsome uniform, Cadet.

A pause

There's a man in it.

CADET

Yes, sir. That's Mr. Stuart. *General* Stuart. My people know him. I'll join his troop!

EUGENE

Handsome fellow. Ask him why he doesn't shave the beard.
He returns the picture.
Winningly
Got a girl, Cadet?

CADET

Blushing
Yes, sir.

EUGENE

She'd like the uniform, too, eh?

CADET

Laughing
Yes, sir.
There is a pause.

EUGENE

I'm going to ask you a very personal question, Cadet.

CADET

Yes, sir.

EUGENE

People who go to war are sometimes wounded.
Steadily and mercilessly
Sometimes, Cadet, they are even . . .

[33]

CADET

Quickly, with a slight gasp

Oh, yes, I know, sir.

EUGENE

Ah, you've thought of that. Good. Now, Cadet, if you should be wounded, where would you prefer the wound to be?

There is a pause.

CADET

In a hesitant tone

Why sir . . . the leg or the arm, I suppose.

EUGENE

I see.

Smoothly

A clean hole, Cadet—no bone.

CADET

With a slight shudder

No, sir.

EUGENE

And if you should be . . . killed?

CADET

Very slowly

Why, sir, *here* . . . or *here*.

He taps his head and breast.

EUGENE

Exactly.

With irony which is not noticed

Face to the foe.

ACT ONE

CADET

With enthusiasm

Yes, sir. In front of all the Cadets . . . leading the charge.
There is a pause.

EUGENE

Yes, exactly. And . . . otherwise, Cadet?
The CADET *does not answer, but he makes a quick
spasmodic gesture, with his hands and turns away.
His shoulders heave once.*

CADET

In a muffled unsteady voice

Then, do you think, sir?

EUGENE

With sudden fierce harshness

Of course not, you little fool. For a gentleman.
With a great cry

Only the peasants get it in the guts. For you, Cadet, there
is only gracefulness. God is a great romancer. He'll save
your prettiness.
Music is played. The CADET *lowers his head and
weeps.*

EUGENE

Speaking in a voice now filled with tenderness

Go back to your dance, Cadet. There will be gray dawns,
hereafter. Tonight you are young; and you can never die.
The CADET *goes out in the direction of the music.
Bugles are blown. The Negro,* TOD, *opens the door.*
MRS. RAMSAY *enters. She is a woman just past fifty,*

with hair which has grayed quite beautifully; to emphasize her sincere, but gravely calculated emotionalism, she employs a tiny lace handkerchief before her mouth as she comes.

Now, Mother, what's the matter?

MRS. RAMSAY

My son! I have found you!

EUGENE

Oh, is that all? And have you searched long, mother— under the rugs, perhaps, and in all the chests?

MRS. RAMSAY

Ah. Gene, my little boy—

EUGENE

Mother, I am touched.

MRS. RAMSAY

I wonder if you can know, Gene, what a mother's feelings are at a time like this.

EUGENE

No, Mother, I cannot. But I am curious. Will you go on?

MRS. RAMSAY

To think that my little son—
She uses her handkerchief again.

EUGENE

Encouragingly

Yes, Mother, I am waiting. "To think that your little son—"

ACT ONE

MRS. RAMSAY

Who used to prattle at my knee.

EUGENE

I beg your pardon? Who used to do what?

MRS. RAMSAY

To prattle at my knee.

EUGENE

Oh, come, Mother. You must be fair, you know. I never did that.

MRS. RAMSAY

Positively

Yes, of course you did, Gene! All children do.

EUGENE

Then, Mother, you should have prevented me. Prattling is a very filthy habit.

MRS. RAMSAY

Oh, Gene, Gene! How can you joke with me tonight— when I am giving so much?

There is a pause.

EUGENE

Pardon me, Mother. You say you are giving a great deal tonight?

MRS. RAMSAY

Yes, Gene.

EUGENE

I do not quite understand, Mother. What is it that you are giving?

[37]

MRS. RAMSAY

A husband and two sons.

There is another pause.

EUGENE

Oh! Yes, I think I see . . . Have you told the General?

MRS. RAMSAY

Shocked

Gene! How can you! My son, I do not know you any more. Why must you make a jest of this?

EUGENE

After a moment

Mother.

MRS. RAMSAY

Yes.

EUGENE

Am I to understand that I am one of the sons you are giving?

MRS. RAMSAY

Gene! What are you saying? I have only two sons.

A pause

EUGENE

Thoughtfully

Yes. I think I see. Then you feel you are giving me, Mother?

MRS. RAMSAY

Yes.

Very proudly

[38]

But I give you gladly, Gene. I thank God it is in my power to make this gift to our cause.

A pause

EUGENE

Pardon me, Mother, but aren't you being a little too generous—shall I say extravagant—with your gifts?

MRS. RAMSAY

With a wounded cry

Gene!

EUGENE

Yes, Mother. But after all, it is my life you are giving, isn't it?

MRS. RAMSAY

Ah, Gene, I would offer my own gladly, but we women can only wait.

EUGENE

Very trying, I'll admit, Mother, but comparatively safe. To be quite frank, Mother, I have a sort of proprietary interest in my own hide which you so generously are offering up to the careful inspection of an enemy who will not hesitate to shoot it full of holes.

MRS. RAMSAY

Deeply shocked

Gene. You, a Ramsay, dare to think of your own safety at a time like this?

EUGENE

A time like this? But pardon me, Mother; isn't this a very good time to think of one's safety? What kind of an ass would I be if I didn't think of it now?

MRS. RAMSAY

In a low voice—but hoarsely

Gene, Gene! Then you are lost—quite lost?

EUGENE

Long, long ago, dear Mother, I wandered out of Arcady. And never may I find the path that takes me back again.

MRS. RAMSAY

I do not understand you, Gene.

EUGENE

You do not know me, Mother. I have no interest in your wars.

MRS. RAMSAY

Indignantly

My war! Gene, *our* war! Is it not your war as well?

EUGENE

No, Mother, love! Wipe the star dust from your eyes. I have no interest in your war. I shall never, never learn to be shot gracefully.

> *Music is played; very fully rich, heavy music, which fills the house with melody*

I heard music then, Mother.

ACT ONE

In a low voice

Are you mad? Gene!

EUGENE

Insistently

But do you hear the music, Mother?

MRS. RAMSAY

In a low, desperate voice

What are you saying, son? The music is very loud!

EUGENE

You are quite wrong, Mother. It is very faint, and very far,
as if it came from a forest, dimly.

> *Enter* RALPH *with the girl,* MARGARET, *the daughter
> of* PATTON. . . . *She is white, slender, beautiful; her
> coiled, black hair is full of little winking lights; it is a
> heavy crown above her white small face, and her dress
> is all of white, and on the small cupped hollow of her
> throat there is a jewelled cameo.* RALPH *is a fair,
> blond fellow two years younger than* EUGENE, *and
> handsome enough in well-cut uniform.*

MRS. RAMSAY

*With a last despairing appeal and a gesture of the
hands*

Eugene! Your brother.

EUGENE

Yes, thank you, Mother. I remember him. We were lads
together. Not a hair is out of place.

[41]

MRS. RAMSAY

Ralph—he is your brother! You must speak to him for our sake.

RALPH

Yes, Mother.

MRS. RAMSAY

For the family—for—for everything.

EUGENE

Come, Mother, all is not lost. There is always Ralph—the Last of the Mohicans, you know.

RALPH

With gentle sternness
Leave us, Mother.

EUGENE

Ah, I perceive that men's work is ahead.

RALPH

I shall speak with you in a moment, sir.

EUGENE

Humbly
Thank you, sir.

MRS. RAMSAY

For *my* sake, Ralph—
She makes a gesture of entreaty and goes out.

EUGENE

And now, Sir Galahad, what is it to be—

RALPH

You forget, sir, that there is a lady present.

EUGENE

Pardon me.

He peers closely at MARGARET.

Yes, she does have the appearance of a lady. Besides, I have never felt her leg. However, one can never be too sure, you know.

RALPH

Fiercely

Damn you, Gene!

EUGENE

Chidingly

Oh, Ralph, before a lady! But there, I remember her when she was not a lady.

RALPH

Take care, sir—

EUGENE

She did her hair in pigtails. I've pulled them often.

MARGARET

Softly

I remember, Gene.

EUGENE

You touch me, Margaret.

More brusquely

And now, Ralph, what have you to say?

RALPH

Don't you think you could show your mother—

EUGENE

Our mother, Ralph. One should be exact even in the details.

RALPH

Don't you think you might show her some consideration tonight—

EUGENE

And who are you, Ralph—my mother's attorney?

RALPH

In a low voice—but very angrily

You are behaving like a thug—you are trying deliberately to make a laughing stock of yourself and your family.

EUGENE

Yes? And you don't approve? But why, Ralph? You shine all the brighter by comparison. You should thank me for setting you off to such advantage—the true courtier, obedient son, dutiful————

RALPH

Where did you get that uniform—from the tentmaker?

MARGARET

Oh, Ralph! To your brother!

EUGENE

Significantly

At any rate, my hat will fit.

ACT ONE

RALPH

Hotly

Let's hope your sword does, too.

MARGARET

Ralph!

EUGENE

But pardon me, are you going to use anything so modern as a sword in this war? I thought, perhaps, that you had decided on a bow and arrow, or a lance, or a battle ax, or whatever found favor in the age of chivalry.

> RALPH *makes a sudden fierce movement toward* EUGENE, *but* MARGARET *places herself in front of him, her hands upon his arms.*

MARGARET

Ralph—Gene—you are brothers!

RALPH

Turning away quickly—and in a low tone

I had forgotten!

EUGENE

No, Ralph. Not 'I had forgotten' but 'True! I had forgotten!' That gives it the final touch, you see. Always with the manner, my boy.

RALPH

With a frank and manly gesture of the hand

I, for one, am willing to let bygones be bygones.

MARGARET

Gene! You must take his hand—you will be separated; perhaps . . .

Her voice sinks.

—you will not see each other for a long time.

EUGENE

With enthusiasm

I had not thought of that! Then this war has some advantages, after all. My dear Ralph, give me your hand.

He seizes Ralph's hand and pumps it vigorously.
Music is played.

RALPH

To MARGARET

There is the music; the dance is mine, I think—

MARGARET

It is yours, yes.

EUGENE

And are there none for me, lady?

MARGARET

Turning on him in white fury

You never asked!

EUGENE

Softly, but with mockery

Yes, lady. But you never heard—you are so far away from me—

ACT ONE

RALPH

With dignity

Let us go, Margaret.

They move slowly toward the door.

MARGARET

To RALPH *at the door, patting his arm gently, hurriedly*

Yes, dear, I will meet you in a moment.

Quickly

My cameo—it is unfastened.

He goes out.

Slowly, to EUGENE *who stands, half-leaning against the table, his dark face twisted in a somber smile; his dull black eyes smoldering with light*

A pause

EUGENE

With a movement of his hand

So far above me, lady. Do you see—up there!

MARGARET

In a small, low whisper of entreaty

Gene! Gene!

EUGENE

Cupping his hands around his mouth, and calling faintly, as if far away

Are you there, lady?

[47]

MANNERHOUSE

Desperately

Gene!

*She goes out to join the others at the dance. He goes
out under the window.*

Bugles are sounded in the camp.

*There comes a man from the darkness, who stands
and knocks hesitantly against the portal. In the dim
light in which he stands, it can be seen that his dress
is common and his body meager; and that his face
is small, narrow, mean and pinched, half-covered
by a straggly unkempt mustache and unshaven beard.
And as he stands there he flenses constantly with the
stubby nails of one blunt hand the skin on the back
of the other, and one notices that this awful hand
is scaly and unclean.*

The Negro, TOD, *appears with stealthy speed and
looms with open menace over the little man, whose
name is* PORTER.

PORTER

Evenin', Tod. Is Mistah Ramsay heah?

TOD

In a low savage growl

You means the gennul.

PORTER

Affably

That's right, Tod.

[48]

TOD

He's in, but he cain't see yo'. They's big goin's-on heah
tonight.

PORTER

Pleadingly

Jes' for a little spell, Tod. Tell him h'it's jes' fer a minnit.

TOD

He cain't se yo', I says.

PORTER

With sudden fierceness

Now, heah, you let me in.

*He attempts to force himself into the room, but the
old Negro thrusts him back with one gaunt arm.
The little man withdraws like a cornered rat; he re-
treats a step and draws stealthily from one pocket a
large knife, which he opens, and advances softly upon
the Negro. He makes a rapid lunge with the knife;
his arm is checked in mid-air with the speed of a cat
by the old Negro who disarms him with a single deft
twist of his hand. They come to grips; the little man
is pinioned like a futile toy in the mighty grip of the
savage. Words pour from his contorted mouth in a
filthy stream.*

PORTER

I done had enough of yo' lip. I ain't goin' to stand for no
mo', nigger. Damned dirty nigger! Black bastards—I hate
niggers.

The GENERAL *enters the room.*

GENERAL

Sharply

Tod!

PORTER

I told him I wa'nt goin' to stand fer his back talk!

GENERAL

Release Mr. Porter.

TOD *releases the man.*

PORTER

Mr. Ramsay—

TOD

With a quick movement

Gennul, I says—

PORTER

You damn nigger!

TOD

With infinite loathing

White trash!

GENERAL

That will do, Tod.

TOD

I told him, Mister Ramsay—

GENERAL

Checking him

In a moment!

To TOD

ACT ONE

Leave us, Tod.

TOD *goes out.*

PORTER

When I asked for you, he wan't goin' to let me in.

GENERAL

I shall punish him if he has been insolent. No doubt he thought he was doing his duty in keeping you out. As you know, this is our last night at home—

PORTER

Eagerly

Yes, sir. That's what I come to see yo' about.

GENERAL

Pointedly

We are very busy, Porter.

PORTER

In open entreaty

Only a minnit, Mister Ramsay—

He gulps and flenses his hand nervously.

GENERAL

Sharply

Yes, Porter.

PORTER

I have a boy, Mister Ramsay.

GENERAL

Yes. He is enlisted in the regiment, I believe.

[51]

PORTER

Eagerly

Yes, sir. That's what I came to see yo' about.

A pause

GENERAL

Well, Porter?

PORTER

I don't know how I'm goin' to git along without that boy, Mister Ramsay—me nor the ole woman, neither. What with the flood, an' the crops late—I need that boy bad, Mister Ramsay.

GENERAL

His cause and his country—the South—need that boy, Porter.

PORTER

Yes, sir. But someone's got to work the farms, ain't they? Sojers got to have victuals, Mister Ramsay, an' my boy's not cut out for sojerin'.

GENERAL

Did he tell you that, Porter?

A pause

PORTER

Bitterly

Him! What's he know! They're all damn fools at twenty!

GENERAL

May their number increase, then! I can do nothing for you, Porter. You come to me with an unworthy and dishonora-

ble request at a time when your cause requires the loyal
services of every man.

PORTER

With rising passion

It ain't my war, Mister Ramsay. Nor my boy's neither.
Why must he be sent way off som'ers to Virginny? What's
Virginny got to do with hit! Let 'em come down heah, if
they want, and I'll shoulder a gun with the best of 'em.

GENERAL

Your country's battles are your battles, wherever they may
be fought—here or in Virginia.

PORTER

Rising with a passionate movement

No, by God! Hit ain't my war, for all your talk. I don't
fight for yore niggers, Mister Ramsay—damn dirty niggers
who don't think me fit to wipe their feet on.

GENERAL

Coldly

That will do! I can do nothing for you!

PORTER

No, but you can take my boy. Hit ain't my war, Mister
Ramsay, I don't own no niggers. I don't live in a house like
this'n. No, by God!

GENERAL

Sharply

Tod!

TOD *appears miraculously and advances on* PORTER,

[53]

who backs away in nervous fury, flensing his hands as he goes.

GENERAL

Show Mr. Porter out!

PORTER

With a mad cry, extending his blunt hands in impotent fury

Christ! Christ!

GENERAL

With cold and implacable disgust, not glancing at the man

Since you seem destitute of honor, I shall give you payment for the sacrifice which other men have made without reward.

PORTER *stops nervously and continuing to flense his scaly hand, stares with fixed interest at the* GENERAL. *The* GENERAL, *in an even inflexible tone:*

The land you till is my land. The house in which you live belongs to my estate; the food you eat, and the air you breathe are mine as well. To you, your heirs, and your inheritors, now and forever, I give outright, without reservation, that land, food, house and air. It is yours.

PORTER

In a hoarse, unbelieving whisper

Give? Did yo' say *give*?

GENERAL

Give. It is your payment.

[54]

ACT ONE

PORTER

In the same hoarse whisper
Will yo' put h't on paper—to do hit legal?

GENERAL

Coldly
It shall be put on paper.

PORTER

With a queer twisted smile, advancing a step or two
I'll shake hands with yo' on hit.

The GENERAL stares at the terrible hand and shudders slightly.

GENERAL

Turning away suddenly
Good evening, sir.

PORTER continues to flense his hand. TOD bears down on him fiercely. The man backs out, but as he goes, he devours the room—its walls and its furnishings with malevolent and greedy eyes; and just before he disappears in darkness he raps gently against the great white column to his right.

TOD crosses the room and goes out.

EUGENE enters from outside.

EUGENE

Saluting with a drunken flourish
In the beginning, General, was the manner.

GENERAL

This is no time for drunken humor, Gene. Tonight you were observed drinking with four of the commonest en-

listed men in the regiment. You command not even the respect of your own men; you are the butt of their jokes—
For the first time EUGENE *winces.*

EUGENE

Yes, General, you yourself have called me a clown. And what's a clown for if not to make men laugh.

GENERAL

I grow old, Eugene; but the pride of my breed is in me.
His voice sinks. A pause
And yet, with you—

EUGENE

It seems to fail.

GENERAL

It seems to fail.
A pause; then with a deep, hurt cry
Where is your pride! Your sense of honor?

EUGENE

What is honor? A word.

GENERAL

A fine word.

EUGENE

And he who had it died on Wednesday. Sir, I am Falstaff without the belly.

GENERAL

And I have lost you, then?

EUGENE

I have grown tired of lace and tinsel.

GENERAL

You have never learned to love them.

EUGENE

Perhaps I learned and have forgotten. But a road leads back if you will follow it. This is a real thing.

GENERAL

In a low voice, as clear as an old bell

Tinsel and lace are real. Men have died for less; men will die for no more—yes, and soon.

EUGENE

And it is for that I must die like a clown—with a plume in my hat.

GENERAL

No. You describe the death of a gentleman.

EUGENE

With a desperate movement

I had expected that! And is that all—to do things grandly, with a manner?

GENERAL

Sir, when I die, I hope I shall make a huge gesture.

EUGENE *turns away swiftly, and begins to laugh terribly, controlling himself presently by clamping one hand upon his mouth.*

[57]

EUGENE

Gasping

O God! O God! O God! A good laugh, isn't it?
He moves toward the window and the dark.

GENERAL

Where are you going, Gene?

EUGENE

Thickly, groping with his hands
Anywhere—to the dark!

GENERAL

No; for you must talk with me tonight, my son.

EUGENE

Turning slowly
Not tonight with you, or ever. It is not possible.

GENERAL

You do not know me, Gene.

EUGENE

I admire your courage. I respect your character. I trust you.

GENERAL

And you do not know me.

EUGENE

I have lost my way—I cannot find you.

GENERAL

And you pity the old man who cannot see? Who cannot
understand?

ACT ONE

EUGENE

I have never said that, General.

GENERAL

Where blows the wind, Eugene?
> *There is a pause.*

EUGENE

> *In a low tone*

I cannot tell you that. But this I know: the wind is up: one
ship is sailing to a far, strange port.

GENERAL

> *With infinite sadness and tenderness*

And you believe in harbors at the end?

EUGENE

With all my heart. With all my heart.

GENERAL

Poor boy! Your harbor is around you, here and now.

EUGENE

> *Quietly*

You are mistaken, General. Not now, not here; not mine.

GENERAL

Yes, yours, and mine. You mad young fool! I give you
proof of this our kingdom, and you ride tilting at the moon.

EUGENE

Our kingdom?

GENERAL

This house, this hill, those fertile fields.

EUGENE

And just beyond the gates—the rabble.

GENERAL

This is my house—this is my kingdom. And that is all that matters. Who cares what is beyond the gates!

EUGENE

In a low, barely audible voice
Beyond the gates perhaps is—God!
Softly. There is a pause.

GENERAL

Ah—h! But never, never, boy.

EUGENE

As before
Yes, General. Out there with all his people.
A pause
I do not record a religious conviction, General. My feeling is purely geographic.

GENERAL

No, above, not with them. God is a great gentleman.

EUGENE

And of our kind! How convenient it is to have God in our own back yard, with all in its proper order.

GENERAL

Steadily
Yes, Gene, with all in its proper order.

ACT ONE

EUGENE

With a desperate movement

Come, General! Do you think God grows cotton?

GENERAL

I know that he is with me against all my enemies.

EUGENE

Eternal partisan!

GENERAL

Would you serve a King who wasn't?

EUGENE

And a Soldier in our war, as well?

GENERAL

Quite true.

EUGENE

Then let Him serve your cause. But why must I?

GENERAL

No, Gene, I cannot tell you that.

EUGENE

Desperately

Then, in God's name, General, give me reasons of your own.
Give me a sign. What is it you believe in?

There is a pause. Bugles are sounded.

GENERAL

You shall have it—the creed of an ancient.

There is a pause; then he begins in a low clear voice.

I believe in God, in Hell and Heaven; and, in my House; in

[61]

a great ladder of things on which it rests. I believe in heroes and hero worship; in men and in masters; in the inequality of all things and all people. I believe in the value of men, and in the beauty and virtue of women, in gallantry, grace, and a sensitive personal honor! I believe in truth, goodness, and beauty; in the preservation of my order of things, and in a society which has for its purpose the preservation of ladies and gentlemen, whom God ever cherishes, loves, and protects. Amen.

EUGENE

That is your gospel.

GENERAL

My Creed.

EUGENE

Founded upon the enslavement of men like us—

GENERAL

Quickly

No! No!

EUGENE

Of men, who but for the grace of your own God might own the fields we make them till; might hold the reins above us.

GENERAL

That is wild and foolish talk, Eugene.

EUGENE

And so we must fight to keep our rights of bondage?

ACT ONE

GENERAL

No! Do you think a war—a simple, stupid, bloody war—
will ruin slavery?

EUGENE

If we lose—

GENERAL

We lose. But slavery is eternal, slavery of field and house
may go down to slavery of mill and wheel. And that in turn
may go down to slavery of another baser sort—the slavery
of a mob to itself—to Rebellion, Rebellion, Rebellion.

EUGENE

His eyes afire
Yes, General! To Rebellion.

GENERAL

There is no virtue in it.

EUGENE

It is excellent and wise—always. I speak for others, General.

GENERAL

Ah, boy! Blind, blind rebel!

EUGENE

No, General, not I.
A pause
But you, General.

GENERAL

Surprised
How's that? What do you mean, boy?

[63]

EUGENE

Panting

That braid upon your sleeve—Are you not a rebel, too?

GENERAL

No, Gene. I am a defender of things established.

EUGENE

You are a rebel, General, and I do not know you.

GENERAL

Do you think, then, you young fool, with all your dreams and your speeches, that you will abolish our way of life? Come, Eugene, slaves are not made—they are born. Win a war, publish a proclamation, make a law! Can you legislate mind into the skull of a savage? Strength into the arm of a weakling? Heart into the breast of a coward? Can you change this?

Bugles are blown. A pause.

EUGENE

General I do not believe in change. My mother gave birth to me when I was a thousand years old. You are quite wrong about me. I have no reforms; I have no progressions; I would save nothing. I believe only in endings.

GENERAL

Why come, this is a very passionate fidelity to death. I have misjudged you. What would you then, Eugene?

EUGENE

Sir, I would have an ending to all things, for I am tired of loneliness.

ACT ONE

GENERAL

Loneliness?

EUGENE

Of loneliness, my ghost. For I am living in a world where all the ghosts are people; all the people ghosts.

With a great cry

You do not know me, General. I am an ancient man, and I must find my way back to my shades again.

He goes swiftly toward the window, and would pass, but he strikes his head against the edge of the lowered sill.

GENERAL

You are too tall, Eugene. Where would you go?

EUGENE

Where a tall man must; I shall come to my house and my home again to find the doors a little taller and the windows high.

GENERAL

I no longer believe in growth, Eugene.

EUGENE

General, you have lived in this house so long that you remember all the chairs when they were nothing but little stools. I am too tall for that. I remember all the stools when they were chairs.

A pause. Bugles are blown.

Why, then if this is so, we are united. I salute you. The ends of the earth are met.

[65]

GENERAL

No, the ends of the earth are never met, and you must greet me from afar.

EUGENE

Your gates are fastened on the world; the world is pressing in.

GENERAL

I must preserve my kingdom.

EUGENE

Your kingdom will vanish in coils of smoke. There must be edges—nothing more.

GENERAL

I must preserve my kingdom! If I can. I will not change it.

EUGENE

You are a very ancient man as well.

> The GENERAL *inclines his head slowly and gravely.*
> *Bugles are blown.*

GENERAL

And now the time grows short, and we must go—I on my way, and you on yours.

> *A pause*

EUGENE

> *In a low voice*

I—on mine?

GENERAL

Yes, Gene. For you shall have no other Gods above your own, and now you know where mine direct. Go where the wind may blow you, boy. Follow your fates to the uttermost part. I am an ancient man, and I shall not prevent you. But tonight when I am gone to war, I charge you, you must go up to your room and take those regimentals off, and leave this house; it is strange to you, and shelters you no longer.

EUGENE

Inclining his head

I have decided!

GENERAL

Then, go your ways, boy. God be with you.

EUGENE

The ends of the earth are met. Our ways are one.

GENERAL

What do you mean?

EUGENE

I go with you. I think I see you now, for the first time; and there's a halo round your head.

GENERAL

With a deep laugh

Idolatry.

EUGENE

I follow the man and not the cause: and serve the man so long as he may live. For I shall go with you, my general, striking a blow for my own disbelief, even though it leads me up the streets of hell at noon.

[67]

GENERAL

Your service is accepted as it is given—honestly.

Bugles are sounded.

Our time is short. Come, boy, come.

They begin to leave the room.

EUGENE

As they go

I heard a fish story, yesterday.

GENERAL

Absently

Yes?

EUGENE

A man on a creek four hundred miles from the sea caught a sea bass.

GENERAL

The story is absurd.

EUGENE

No. Perhaps the rivers are flowing backward.

Within the house there is a swelling movement of the music which ends. Bugles are sounded in the camp. The voices and the mirth of all the guests are heard, coming closer.

GENERAL

"Even though it leads me up the streets of hell at noon."
Why this is excellent, splendid! You are learning the language; the gestures should follow naturally.

ACT ONE

VOICES

Young and beautiful and joyous, near the door

The toast, General. The toast.

OTHER VOICES

Older, farther off, sadder

Yes, yes. The toast, General.

RALPH *enters with* MRS. RAMSAY.

RALPH

The guests are all ready.

A confused hum of voices

GENERAL

Calling

Tod!

TOD *and* BYNUM, *a very black young Negro, appear
with wine glasses upon a tray.*

Laughter far and near within the house

MANY VOICES

The toast!

The GENERAL, *a wine glass poised between his fingers,
goes to the left door which* BYNUM *opens for him and
begins to speak to the guests—who are unseen save
for* MARGARET, *the* MAJOR *and a few cadets who
cluster around the* GENERAL—*but audible.*

GENERAL

Ladies and gentlemen, my good friends, fellow cadets.

Laughter and cheers

[69]

I could drink to so many glorious things: to youth, to beauty—there's so much of it around me here—

Applause and laughter

—to youth and courage in these gallant young cadets who are going forth—

Applause

MAJOR

Wheeling in excitement

One hundred and seventeen under nineteen.

EUGENE

What a head for figures you have, Major!

GENERAL

Or even more might I drink—

A CADET

Why not to our cause, General?

GENERAL

And to our cause, my boy. But tonight before you go, before you dance again, I shall ask you to drink with me a health that has grown old in the mouth of every master of this family. Good friends, I give you: To the house!

ALL

Seen and unseen

To the house!

They drink. EUGENE *drinks and hurls his glass upon the floor. There is a great murmur of surprise and disapproval.*

[70]

ACT ONE

An ancient custom—that a health be not repeated!

GENERAL

Quietly
And even now?

EUGENE

It holds, General.
Music begins.

GENERAL

And, now, let us dance again, while there is time.
Bugles are sounded. The guests are gone to their dancing.

EUGENE

And let us save the last for———?

GENERAL

For glory.

EUGENE

For death.
The GENERAL *dances with* MRS. RAMSAY *and they go out.*

RALPH

Approaching MARGARET
And once again.

MARGARET

To RALPH
No more, my dear, tonight.

[71]

MANNERHOUSE

RALPH

To MARGARET

Once more, my dear, once more.

MARGARET

In a low voice, steadily, gently

For you there are no more, my dear.

He goes out blindly.

EUGENE

And is that how you treat a knight?

MARGARET

The dances are almost done.

EUGENE

We may not dance forever, Margaret.

MARGARET

In a low, faint whisper—staring straight before her

If we only could!

A pause—a whisper—then:

Eugene!

EUGENE

I hear bells. How pure a woman are you, lady?

A pause. He seizes, holds, embraces her; he kisses her upon the mouth.

MARGARET

Eugene—

EUGENE

Why, this is a good season for fruit. Are your melons ripe, lady?

He thrusts his hand into her breast; his knee insinuates itself between her legs; her body twists; it writhes slowly and stubbornly in a futile and resentful ecstasy, and slides in heavily to rest against him.
Coldly

To arms! To arms! Where are the brothers of Lucrece?

MARGARET

Comatose; whispering
I do not care; I am not ashamed.

EUGENE

And no one comes. I should have thought a thousand swords would leap—oh, Burke, forgive me! But, soft you now, I feel the fair Ophelia. Yes, there's a pure heart here: It has a church-bell rhythm in its beating. Purity, can you say "God," can you say "Mother"?—oh, then, we'll be married: the parson will bless us, my mother will kiss you, a company of brave and honest knights will guard you to our bed, and we shall have our cake and eat it until we're fifty. We shall be fruitful, lady, and get much praise for it. How pleasant a thing it is to be holy. What a dull and difficult life all sinners have!

MARGARET

Eugene, I do not care. You are my knight.

EUGENE

Your knight. Why, then, it is fair that I should have from you a token.

[73]

MARGARET

What you will, Eugene.

EUGENE

In older days, the lady gave a glove. But that was before they learned the art of wearing drawers. Give me a ruffle for the love of God.

MARGARET

This foulness passes you like muddy water over stone. It can do no harm to you.

EUGENE

What does it matter if you feel a lady's leg, so long as her heart is pure?

MARGARET

I know you as you are, Eugene.

EUGENE

And you believe in me.

MARGARET

With a passion greater than that of those who have never believed at all, or of them who believe forever.

EUGENE

With a fierce cry

Ghost! Ghost! You have slain me!

A pause. He comes nearer.

Your hair is dark as coiled smoke, Margaret. You are a great perfume, and I am drunken on you.

MARGARET

And you must dance with me, Eugene.

EUGENE

I cannot hold a phantom in my arms—oh, stay a minute.
Move, my ghost—you will be gone like mist.

MARGARET

Oh, dance this once with me, Eugene.

EUGENE

And would you give your dances to a clown?

MARGARET

No clown! But to a brave and gallant knight.

EUGENE

A knight—and have you seen his armor?
> *He fingers, with a twisted smile, the buttons of his clumsy jacket.*

MARGARET

You are my brave, my gallant knight, and if you go disguised today, I know that it's a wicked spell, and that you'll be my own tomorrow when you come riding down to Camelot. I was a child when I first saw you, and I took you for my little God. Once you hurt yourself—I don't know how—and when you came to me I drew you down on me and gave you comfort. Others will look at you, perhaps, and see a man, and judge you as men are judged—

EUGENE

God save me!

MARGARET

But I—you are my little God, and all you do is wise. I can't go on—I can't say why or how—but you are good, you are beautiful. I love you.

She lays her hands lightly upon his arms.

Dearest! Dearest!

EUGENE

Your little God is clay up to his knees but he thinks he loves you, ghost. But that is just a little empty thing. You are in his blood like wine; you stir a leaping madness in his brain.

He kisses her, and the music swells and fills the house.

A pause. In a quiet, altered voice

That was the manner. Very well. Shall I cough, then, in the middle of a line, refuse to cross my *t*'s or dot my *i*'s? Ah, idiot pattern. Is there a victory in perverseness? Yes; I shall speak then in the manner, which renews itself forever.

MARGARET

In a low whisper

My little God, I love you!

EUGENE

Your eyes are closed, and I could drink oblivion upon your mouth. I feel your breath upon me, and the pressure of your breast; and I am mad with love of you, my ghost. My God, my God, how real a dream may be! While we were yet alive, my ghost—

MARGARET

Ah, it is real, and we are living, Gene.

ACT ONE

EUGENE

A moment more, my ghost—before I lose you.

MARGARET

You shall not lose me, Gene.
Bugles are blown.

EUGENE

That was the world! And in this night I have won and lost
a perishable thing—the love of a lady from the ghostly
world.

MARGARET

You will return, my dear.

EUGENE

Yes, lady; but you will be gone.

MARGARET

No, no, I will be here for you, always, always.

EUGENE

You will be gone, my ghost, along with your courts and
castles—gone into smoke and dreams, far away to elf land.
*Bugles are sounded faintly on the road. The music
rises to a mighty rhythm.*
Kiss me, my dear—my little ghost. You will be gone, and I
must die of hunger.
He kisses her slowly on the mouth.

MARGARET

Then I shall die of cold.

EUGENE

This is the Alpha and Omega, the first and the last, the beginning and the end.

A VOICE

Outside

Eugene!

EUGENE

I am ready.

MARGARET

Quickly, entreatingly

Not yet, my dear, not yet.

EUGENE

Margaret, good-by.

He kisses her and they go out in different directions.
The music dies; and the guests are departing. There
is a sound of sorrow in their voices; the moon has
wheeled far down the sky. A CADET *comes with a*
girl into the moonlight and kisses her. He plunges
into darkness and is gone. She comes again into the
house. RALPH *enters the room with his mother.*

RALPH

I must go now, Mother.

MRS. RAMSAY

God bless you, son, and save you for me.

RALPH

Good-by, Mother.

He kisses her and goes. The GENERAL *enters wearing*
his sword.

MRS. RAMSAY

I am afraid. For the first time, I doubt.

ACT ONE

GENERAL

Gently

Come, my dear. Afraid? And in this room?

MRS. RAMSAY

The world is crumbling at my feet. My life drops to the river like mined earth.

GENERAL

You must endure whatever comes.

MRS. RAMSAY

The worst?

GENERAL

Take heart: We shall yet be saved.

MRS. RAMSAY

I doubt, God knows.

A pause

Where is our boy?

GENERAL

Coming—like a soldier now.

EUGENE *enters the room splendidly uniformed.*

Why, that is handsome, boy.

MRS. RAMSAY

Eugene!

EUGENE

Half jestingly

And yet again, Mother.

GENERAL

Sharply

The true Eugene.

EUGENE

Quietly

Yes, General.

GENERAL

Go say a word for sentiment.

EUGENE

Going to her swiftly and looping his arms gracefully around her

Mother!

MRS. RAMSAY

With a glad cry

My son! My own true son!

EUGENE

Mother, we must be brave.

He releases himself gently. To the GENERAL

I am ready, sir.

GENERAL

Rubbing his hands gleefully

Why, boy, this is good. Splendid. You learn quickly. Perhaps simply "Lead—I follow," with a simple but appropriate gesture, would be better.

EUGENE

Quickly

You are quite right.

ACT ONE

He embraces his mother again. Releasing himself,
with a simple but appropriate gesture, to the GENERAL

Lead! I follow!

GENERAL

It is magnificent!

MRS. RAMSAY

Quickly

No, no, Eugene. I cannot bear to lose you now just as I
find you. Come, my boy—

EUGENE

Gravely

Then, for a moment, Mother.

They go out.

A VOICE

From the darkness behind the house

Sir!

GENERAL

Yes?

VOICE

I am coming.

Bugles are sounded through the encampment. The
regiment has swung into action. Outside may be heard
the sounds of men and beasts—shouts, cries, low,
sharp commands, the dull creaking of heavy wagons,
and a low even thunder of marching feet from the
road beyond. Small lights swing drunkenly as the

[81]

wagons lurch into the way. The regiment is on the march.

There is a wind about the house; a cloud is driven across the moon. For a moment there is darkness and spouting rain. When the scene lightens the Negro TOD *has entered the room bringing the* GENERAL'S *hat and gauntlets. The* GENERAL, *putting on his gauntlets:*

Tod, I leave the management of my estate in your keeping, to do all things your mistress bids you.

The Negro nods.

You are my good and faithful servant, and I trust you.

The GENERAL *offers* TOD *his gloved hand. The Negro takes it reverently, raises it swiftly to his mouth and lets it fall.*

Deeply stirred

My faithful servant; my good friend.

Somewhere within the house—perhaps within the room—but in the house somewhere, there is a displeasing sound—the sound of a single large drop of water which somewhere forms, swells, develops, and falls at length with an unvarying punctual monotony.

GENERAL

Put out the lights, Tod.

The lights are extinguished. Listening intently

Do you hear, Tod? Water is falling somewhere in the house. There is a leak. Find it and stop it.

[82]

ACT ONE

VOICE

From darkness without

General.

GENERAL

Quickly fastening his gauntlets

Coming, sir. Tod, you understand.

He walks rapidly toward the entrance.

Pausing, before he goes, with a deep breath

And now, gentlemen—

He goes out, followed by TOD.

TOD *returns bearing in one huge long hand a dim lantern. He begins to scan the wall to observe the presence of the water.*

A THIN VOICE

Far and high, howling with malevolent laughter

Snap your fingers, gentlemen.

The Negro begins to circle the room, in a foiled search, with great strides, the dim lantern moving high above his head from one huge hand. Even his pace is quickened, until at length he is circling the room like a great hound, making baffled, snarling noises in his throat. Bugles are sounded, far and thin, from the road.

CURTAIN

Interlude

This is an interlude to be played behind the curtains during the intermission between the first and second acts:

Let there be music and crowd as follows: First, let there be heard a low sound of marching feet, and a low faint sound of music. And let these sounds come nearer, until the feet pass the curtain in loud and even rhythm; and there is brisk, spirited music, with rolling drums and tooting fifes. And let all this again grow faint, until one hears a heavy rumble of the drums and great shouts and cries far off. And let feet pass the curtain again, this time running and disorderly: and let the music return again, this time the song of "Dixie," played as a weary broken tune, stumbling home on blind and crippled feet.

Act Two

Part One

SCENE: *When the curtain rises the stage is quite dark, although through the bars of the shuttered windows the sunlight of a fine April morning is printed on the floor in level rifts. The year is 1865.*

It has rained heavily the night before and in the silence one sound is audible—the sound of the single large drop of water which, perhaps within the room, certainly within the house somewhere, forms, swells, develops, and drops with an unvarying punctual monotone.

TOD *goes to the windows and opens the shutters. The room is flooded with light. For the first time now, it is possible to see a mark of desolation upon the house. The interior has a stained, weathered appearance; upon the columns just beyond the doors the paint has soiled in yellow patches. A sturdy weed has thrust its tendrils round the base of one column.*

Presently, there are steps on the porch and a hesitant, timid knocking at the door. A gay, very black Negro stands at the entrance, grinning sheepishly and rather fearfully, and yet curious, apparently, to note what effect the outrageous and gaudy display of finery,

[87]

as of socks, shoes, shirt, that he wears may produce on TOD. *He is* BYNUM.

BYNUM

Dat you, Tod?

TOD

Pausing slowly

Is you speakin' to me, boy?

BYNUM

Yes, sah. I sho' is!

TOD

Boy, I don't know you.

BYNUM

Is de Marse come?

TOD

What Marse?

BYNUM

Nettled

Marse Will!

TOD

Ominously

I puhsoom you is talkin' of de head of dis hear house—Gennul Ramsay.

BYNUM

You knows who I's talkin' 'bout.

ACT TWO

Looking up slowly

De Marse, says you?

BYNUM

De Marse, says I.

TOD

Uh, uh, boy. You ain't got no Marse. You was too smart, you was.

With scathing contempt

You is a free niggah, you is.

BYNUM

Is Mis' Mary heah?

TOD

She's heah, but you won't be heah long, boy, if she cotch you. Go on boogety-boogety down de road now, lak I tells you. We don't need no black truck heah.

BYNUM *turns unwillingly to go.*

TOD

Recalling him

Wheah'd you get dem clo's, boy?

BYNUM

I's wokkin' on de railroad—dollah a day.

TOD

You'd bettah stick to de railroad, boy. Don't go wearin' dat shirt neah dem bulls in de pastuah. Git along now.

MRS. RAMSAY *comes in with* MARGARET, *who carries flowers.*

[89]

MRS. RAMSAY

Sharply

Who's there, Tod?

TOD

Unwillingly

Dat boy—Bynum.

MRS. RAMSAY

Where is he? Let me see him.

BYNUM *appears grinning sheepishly.*

BYNUM

Mawnin', Mis' Mary.

MRS. RAMSAY

Ironically

Mercy! What a fine gentleman you've become!

BYNUM

Grinning

Yas'm.

MRS. RAMSAY

With dignity

I am told that you have left us, Bynum.

BYNUM

After a pause

Yas'm.

MRS. RAMSAY

Yes? And why are you here now?

BYNUM

To see de Marse.

MRS. RAMSAY

You have no master, Bynum—you have deserted him. Perhaps the time will come when you will be sorry for the way you have treated your good master, the master who was always so kind to you.

BYNUM

Yas'm.

MRS. RAMSAY

Until that time, Bynum, never show yourself around this house again. Really, I don't see how you can look us in the face.

But BYNUM *has been looking steadily at the floor for some time.*

Now you may go.

The Negro BYNUM *goes off with straggling steps. She looks after him, striving hard to control her wounded pride and curiosity.*

Recalling him with an impulsive cry

Bynum!

BYNUM

Returning

Yas'm.

MRS. RAMSAY

Why did you go?

BYNUM

Slowly

Why, I don' know, Mis' Mary. I reckon it was 'case we knowed we could.

He goes.

MRS. RAMSAY

Staring straight before her, in flat intonations

He was always so proud of his hold over them. He said they were his not so much by possession as by love and loyalty. How shall I tell him! How shall I tell him now!

MARGARET

Perhaps he knows.

A pause

MRS. RAMSAY

Margaret, we will never know. We will never know.

Going to TOD *impulsively*

You stayed! Oh, you stayed.

She seizes his huge black hand and presses it. He bows sternly, yet tenderly, and with some embarrassment withdraws his hand.

Briskly, authoritatively

Tod, I want you to remove the cover from the furnishings at once.

TOD begins to draw the linen covers from the furnishings one by one and to fold them neatly.

Faint bugle notes upon the road, and a subdued jingling of bridles and accoutrements

There is no news yet, I suppose?

ACT TWO

MARGARET

No. The roads are mudholes after the rains, and the train is invariably late.

MRS. RAMSAY

Everything is choked up with troops. That causes delay.

MARGARET

Yes.

> *A pause.* TOD *goes out.*

MRS. RAMSAY

Margaret.

MARGARET

> *In a low voice*

It is quite over, dearest.

MRS. RAMSAY

> *With a pleading note*

But there's Johnson!

MARGARET

He must—surrender, the Major says, within a week.

MRS. RAMSAY

> *With a strangled cry*

And we've lost!

MARGARET

> *Gently*

Lost? No, dearest.

> *In a low voice*

This is the time of curly roses, and he is coming.

[93]

MRS. RAMSAY

Sadly

The romance of the business is a little wilted, I'm afraid. I sent three out, my dear, and only two return.

Fiercely

My God would never help such devils! Never!

A pause

MARGARET

While she arranges the flowers in a vase on the table

I keep hearing something, and I don't know what it is.

Bugles sound on the road.

MRS. RAMSAY

The troops are passing on the road, my dear.

MARGARET

This is in the house, I think—Tell me, what is Eugene going to do now? Has he said?

MRS. RAMSAY

Surprised

But surely, you must know we have never had any other plans for Gene than the management of the estate. Neither the General nor I are as young as we once were, and, as you know, a vast estate like this, with hundreds of people upon it—

She stops suddenly, and sways a little.

MARGARET

Gently

You are tired, dearest. Rest awhile.

[94]

ACT TWO

MRS. RAMSAY

My God—why did you ask me that?

MARGARET

For no reason—it was stupid! After what he has seen . . .

MRS. RAMSAY

Triumphantly

Of course! After what he has seen, he will never care to leave!

MARGARET

In a low tone

If I knew!

MRS. RAMSAY

Picking up a book and opening it

I shall leave this volume on the table.

MARGARET

Without looking

Scott, of course.

MRS. RAMSAY

Yes. The General's favorite author.

Turning a few pages

My dear, do you know these lines:

Breathes there a man with soul so dead
Who never to himself hath said:
"This is my own, my native land,"
Whose heart hath ne'er within him burned

As home his footsteps he hath turned,
From wandering on a foreign strand.

Bugles are sounded on the road.

MARGARET

If such there breathe, go mark him well,
For him no minstrel raptures swell.

Yes, I know them quite well. Father has recited them a hundred times. But I am afraid no minstrel rapture will swell today.

Hurried footsteps on the porch

MRS. RAMSAY

I always know your father by the sound of his feet.

The MAJOR *enters, a little fatter and redder, more apoplectic than ever, beautifully groomed, and so tightly buckled that his pendulous little belly swings sturdily from left to right as he comes. He is in his usual panting, stertorous condition of excitement and exertion.*

MARGARET

Father, you wheeze so terribly.

MAJOR

News, Marg, news!

MRS. RAMSAY

Quickly
They are here!

MAJOR

No—the train's late. However, they are on the way.

> MARGARET *goes to the window to observe the road.*

MRS. RAMSAY

I understand you are making plans for the reopening of the Academy.

MAJOR

Oh, yes. I'm quite busy in fact.

MRS. RAMSAY

You expect, I suppose, for a time some decrease in attendance?

MAJOR

Oh, a little, perhaps, a little. Not a great deal, but a little.

MARGARET

I should not be too optimistic, Father. The school has been closed four years, you know.

MAJOR

> *Waving his hand tolerantly*

My dear, I'm afraid you don't understand these matters. School has been closed four years, you say. Quite true. But this school has been established since 1789. Not even a war can disturb such an institution!

MRS. RAMSAY

Of course!

MARGARET

Naturally, it must go on forever!

> *Bugles on the road*

MAJOR

And when they hear of our record—ah, what a story for the new catalog! "In our great struggle against organized bigotry," I have written, "a contest in which we were defeated, but not beaten . . ."

Carriage wheels are heard outside.

MARGARET

They are here!

A sensation. All rush out, the MAJOR *still declaiming vigorously.*

MAJOR

"Until not a single commissioned officer was left, and of the original one hundred and seventeen . . ."

Voices, laughter, greetings outside. TOD *walks rapidly through the room, pulling on a pair of frayed cotton gloves, through whose ragged edges his fingers, now trembling as with ague, protrude. He rushes out.*

EUGENE, *thin almost to emaciation but indurated by four years of open weather and by weeks of fasting on parched corn, to almost an exposure, enters by the window. There is subtle mockery in the angle at which he wears his incredibly battered hat, with its soiled, awkward plume.*

EUGENE

Entering

While I was yet alive—

MARGARET, *fear and disappointment on her face, returns before the others.*

MARGARET

Whispering almost

Gene!

EUGENE

With a flourish of the hat

Most musical of voices, speak again.

MARGARET

Gene!

She touches his sleeve almost in disbelief.

EUGENE

Ah, which of us is the ghost, I wonder?

MARGARET

With a strangled cry, seizing him

Gene! Gene!

EUGENE

So poor a man as Hamlet is. My dear, you will rumple my
uniform.

He loosens her hands, gently.

MARGARET

Where were you! I didn't see you! I was afraid—Oh, Gene,
how did you get here?

EUGENE

Solemnly—looking around carefully

Sh-h—I will tell you: through the window.

MARGARET

But why, Eugene?

EUGENE

Looking around carefully again—in a loud whisper

I couldn't find the door.

In a low voice

It has not grown.

The MAJOR *enters*

The leader of the honored one hundred and seventeen! Major, how are you?

They shake hands.

MAJOR

We are very proud of you, Eugene.

EUGENE

Well, Major, are you ready to admit now that we're beaten?

MAJOR

Defeated, perhaps, but never beaten.

EUGENE

With enthusiasm

Now that's a splendid distinction! Defeated, but never beaten! I suppose there's a difference but my head's not good enough today to see it. Will you remind me of it again next Thursday?

He begins opening drawers in the General's desk.

MARGARET

What do you want, Gene?

EUGENE

I am looking for the family honor. Have you seen it around lately?

[100]

ACT TWO

MARGARET

Be quiet!

EUGENE

It should always be kept under lock and key. I shall be a noble patriot. I shall run for Congress. I believe in bathtubs with the innocent faith of a child.

> *The* GENERAL *and* MRS. RAMSAY *enter. The years of war have bronzed his face, bringing his large craggy features into bolder and more generous relief. It is a face with courage and intelligence enough for anyone or anything.*

MRS. RAMSAY

> *With a cry*

Eugene!

EUGENE

Mother! Yours, yours, yours!
> *He kisses her.*

MRS. RAMSAY

My brave boy!

EUGENE

Tush, Mother. I might even say: Pshaw!

MRS. RAMSAY

God has given you back to me.

EUGENE

You are mistaken: we must always give the Devil his due.

MRS. RAMSAY

Looking at him intently

My poor boy, you are starved.

EUGENE

The result of overeating in the army.

GENERAL

What became of that very excellent old mule in your company, Eugene?

EUGENE

The old boy went to glory weeks ago.

GENERAL

And yet you are hungry?

EUGENE

You see, he was not very large for his age.

He thrusts a hand into his pocket and draws it forth.

Won't someone join me in a handful of parched corn? It's very fattening.

MARGARET

But they feed that to chickens.

EUGENE

Yes, I have learned to cackle like a rooster. Cock-a-doodle-doo!

TOD *appears with glasses on a tray. They are filled with brandy.*

MAJOR

You know, I feel the occasion demands a little toast—

ACT TWO

GENERAL

A toast then—what shall it be? I propose that everyone make a suggestion.

To the MAJOR

Yours?

MAJOR

There is only one—
With a gallant bow
To William and Mary, who have reigned for thirty years:
May they reign for thirty more!

The GENERAL *and his lady make pretty bows.*

MRS. RAMSAY

That is very generous, Major. But today we must not be personal: I want to take a great deal in, you see.

Bugles sound on the road.

GENERAL

And what is yours, my dear?

MRS. RAMSAY

To our glorious past, whose traditions may we always hold in reverence.

EUGENE

To the sword which pierces very far! To the consuming flame. To endings, to endings, to endings.

GENERAL

I like your mother's best.

To MARGARET

And yours, my dear.

Faint singing from the road

MARGARET

Listening

To the soldiers of the world, now and forever, whose business it is to have no fear of death.

EUGENE

It's too poor a business. There's no future in it.

MARGARET

Cynic! But it's true! The General was a soldier, and he is not afraid of death.

EUGENE

I've always been afraid of it—but I'm a philosopher!

GENERAL

Mine is . . .

In a ringing voice

To the house!

EUGENE

Quietly

I'll join you in that one, Father.

MAJOR

Uneasily

I keep hearing something, and I don't know what it is.

EUGENE

Solemnly

Is it a still small voice, Major?

ACT TWO

Raising his glass

Nil Separabit. Nothing shall part us, while this house may stand and take us in its broad, white arms, and give us rest and shelter. I say, God keep such houses, and all the gentle souls who rest in them.

MAJOR

Amen!

EUGENE

Amen! Amen! I, too, have lived in Arcady.

> *Now from the road, there comes a distinct sound—of men who sing old broken songs as their weary bodies swing in the saddles, and of dumb hoofbeats, muffled in the dust, and of reins and spur, and saber, but all so drowsed in the warmth of the sleepy day, so faint, so far remote, that you would say the sounds were elfin from a phantom wood.*

MARGARET

Oh, what is that upon the road?

GENERAL

Cavalry going home—poor boys!

MRS. RAMSAY

How faint! How far away it seems!

MARGARET

Going to the windows

I can see the sun upon their bridles through the hedge. That is all.

[105]

MRS. RAMSAY

The hedges must be trimmed. Once there was a good view of the road.

MAJOR

They should be trimmed.

EUGENE

They should be cut.

GENERAL

They shall stay—I like high hedges.

MARGARET

Looking

How long will they go by, I wonder?

EUGENE

They cannot go by forever, Margaret.

MARGARET

In a low voice, looking out

If they only could! If they only could!

MAJOR

With enthusiasm

What a fine thing it is to see a man upon a horse!

EUGENE

Yes. It sets the horse off to great advantage, doesn't it?

MRS. RAMSAY

To GENERAL

Shall we lunch here, or in the dining room?

ACT TWO

Rather sharply

In the dining room, of course. Let everything proceed according to routine as quickly as possible. That is important.

MRS. RAMSAY

Aside, to MAJOR

He's such an executive!

MAJOR

Oh, superb.

GENERAL

I shall lose no time in getting down to business. There must be letters—

MRS. RAMSAY

In your desk, dear.

GENERAL

No doubt, there is a great deal to do. It will take some time, perhaps.

EUGENE

The best part of a morning, General.

GENERAL

Strikes a bell on the table. TOD *appears.*

Tod, I shall want all my people assembled here.

EUGENE

Quietly

Father!

MRS. RAMSAY

With a cry

Gene!

A swift look passes between them.

GENERAL

Rather sharply

What is it, Gene!

EUGENE

Nothing.

GENERAL

Tell me later, then. Why the devil don't you shave? You can now, you know.

EUGENE

Meekly

It is not allowed, I suppose, for anyone under the rank of General to go in for whiskerage.

GENERAL

Always shave for the servants, my boy. Position demands it. And, for God's sake, throw that hat away.

MARGARET

Oh, Gene, the plume!

EUGENE

Taking it out and giving it to her with a bow

Lady, it is yours. I suggest you have it cleaned before you use it.

ACT TWO

MARGARET

Dramatically
I shall wear it next to my heart.

EUGENE

That will be a ticklish business, I'm afraid.

GENERAL

To TOD
Why was there no one here to meet me, Tod?

MRS. RAMSAY

Quickly
We did not know what time you would arrive, you see.

GENERAL

Oh, of course. I was a bit surprised and hurt, I'll admit.
To TOD
You must tell everyone, then, to be here at two o'clock.

EUGENE

Quietly as before
Father!

GENERAL

In a moment, Gene.

MRS. RAMSAY

In a whisper
Gene, dear—

MARGARET

Please! Please!

GENERAL

Impatiently, To EUGENE

What is it, now?

EUGENE

Nothing. Why don't you take off your sword—you might sit on it and cut yourself.

GENERAL

Please don't interrupt.

To the group

He is quite mad—I've known him for years.

EUGENE

That's long enough to find a fool—a wise man hides more carefully.

GENERAL

To TOD

Do not alarm them, Tod. Tell them I shall keep them all— Do you hear?—

TOD *bows inflexibly.*

GENERAL *triumphantly:*

—that there is no cause for alarm.

TOD *bows sternly.*

And that they must all be here at two o'clock.

TOD *bows.* GENERAL *goes out, followed by* TOD.

MARGARET

To MRS. RAMSAY

I shall help you, then.

They go out other door.

ACT TWO

MAJOR

To EUGENE *who has wandered toward the door*

Eugene, I want to talk with you soon.

EUGENE

By all means.

He wanders out upon the porch

I must tell you about the battle of Saw-tooth Gap, where I led the charge.

Declaiming, as he disappears

There were nineteen of us, I remember, all under one hundred and seventeen. "Forward, my lads," I cried. "We must be in Washington in time for the inauguration."

MAJOR

Smiling

Ah, youth, youth!

EUGENE

Reappearing suddenly

What's that, Major?

MAJOR

Ah, youth, youth!

EUGENE

Thank you, Major; I was just going to say that.

MAJOR

The hope of the world, the glory of the past, the promise of the future. And you are young, Eugene.

EUGENE

Major, you touch me.

[111]

MAJOR

Ah, yes, my boy, you are young, and the future of this world is in your keeping. It is for you young men to mend this broken scheme of things which we, the old, have so grievously mishandled. It is for you, the young, to highly resolve—

EUGENE

That government of the people, for the people, by the people—Why, by God, Major, it is as good as a game.

MAJOR

A game, Eugene?

EUGENE

A very ancient and honorable game; for if you are young it shall be pleasant to name the sins of old men; if you are old it shall be pleasant to confess them.

MAJOR

We have just passed through a terrible war, Eugene.

EUGENE

A very terrible war, Major.

MAJOR

The most horrible war, Eugene. Bleeding from her broken wounds, this nation—

EUGENE

This very great nation, Major.

MAJOR

This very great nation, Eugene.

ACT TWO

EUGENE

This greatest of all great nations, Major; for just as all wars
are the most terrible, so are all nations the greatest and most
powerful; all armies the bravest; and all women the most
beautiful and most virtuous. Major, everything has grown
so great we must prepare for changes.

MAJOR

Yes, Eugene. We are at one of the crises of history; at a
turning point. A great change is before us.

EUGENE

Things can never be the same again, Major. Among other
things, from now on, the moon will rise under your left
elbow and go down in Constantinople; all male children
with red hair who are more than two years old at the time
of their birth, will immediately be given important positions
in the diplomatic service: and young married women will
not acquire a maidenhood until they reach the age of
twenty-eight. Moreover the youth of the world, under my
leadership, will band together for freedom, truth, beauty,
art, and love, and will wage merciless war on hypocrisy,
custom, and tradition: for they have been tricked.

MAJOR

Tricked, Eugene?

EUGENE

Major, not merely tricked, but tr-r-ricked! And by whom?

MAJOR

By whom, Eugene?

EUGENE

Why, by these false, lying, greedy, selfish and murderous old men the world over, who sit around the council tables and cater to their own base self-interests, deluding and deceiving us all the time with fine speeches about loyalty and defense of country. Am I right or am I wrong?

MAJOR

With a certain melancholy pleasure in his voice

Ah, my boy, I fear that you are right. What you say is only too true; we have made a sorry botch of things. And yet, at the price of disillusion, you young men have learned much, Eugene.

EUGENE

Yes, Major. The price we have paid for wisdom is a heavy one, but we have learned. Do you know what I have found?

MAJOR

No, Eugene.

EUGENE

Looking around cautiously

You must not reveal this to anyone, but I have found out what men do to one another when they go to war.

Earnestly

Major, you may believe it if you like, but they shoot one another.

Solemnly

Yes, Major, it is nothing less than wicked. It amounts to

murder. At any rate, its effects upon the nervous system are much the same.

With intensity

Yes, Major, that is what we have found out—we young men.

MAJOR

Ah, youth will not be deceived, I know. Its quick wit, its flaming iconoclasm strike through the armor of old sophistries. The scales have fallen from its eyes.

EUGENE

Exactly, exactly, exactly. We see things now exactly as they are. Look closely in my eyes, if you please, Major.

The MAJOR *does so doubtfully.*

Do you not see hell in them?

Without waiting for a reply

Of course you do, Major. I have come back with hell in my eyes. We always do. And how do we go out to war, Major?

MAJOR

With fire and idealism, Eugene.

EUGENE

With a great deal of fire and idealism, Major. And we invariably come back with hell in our eyes. Major, it is quite as good as a game.

MAJOR

A tragic game, Eugene.

Yes, Major, youth may be deceived, but not for long. For example, it has taken us only four years, by means of our preternaturally sharp intelligence, to discover that war is a very tedious, unpleasant and dangerous business. There is hope in all this. With fair luck we may know enough to come in out of the rain by the time we are eighty.

MAJOR

Sadly

I cannot blame you, boy. Your experience has made you bitter.

EUGENE

With a laugh of fictitious bitterness

God, yes. That was a good laugh, eh, Major? But we are not done with you old fellows, Major. We are going to have something to say about all this before we're through. We shall say, perhaps, that all the men in the world are brothers —all the young men. We are going to write some books and poems about all this. Perhaps we shall even write some plays. I make no promises. We shall burst all old hypocrisies. We shall give traditions a handsome stiff kick in the rump. We shall tell about things exactly as they are. We shall be free.

The faithful dog trots slowly and heavily by.

EUGENE

Stroking the dog

I am very fond of dogs, Major. I have known many different breeds, but chiefly mad dogs.

ACT TWO

MAJOR

He is a faithful animal, Eugene. His emotion at his Master's return today was very touching.

EUGENE

A faithful dog, Major, but an old dog. In his youth, I wonder, was he ever a gay dog?

MAJOR

A gay dog, Gene? How d'ye mean?

EUGENE

With an affected and embarrassed laugh

Oh, you know what I mean, Major. I hardly know how to say it.

MAJOR

No, I don't understand.

EUGENE

Solemnly

I mean, Major, do you think our dog has ever *lived*?

With a vulgar leer

Really lived, Major?

MAJOR

In his youth, perhaps, Gene, when every dog has its day.

EUGENE

In his youth, to be sure. Tameless and swift and proud, like all young things, eh, Major?

MAJOR

Yes, Gene. Like all young things. That is the crown jewel of all life.

With a cry

Give me youth again.

EUGENE

When the dog was young, did he go alone, or did he travel in a pack, Major?

MAJOR

Why, how should I know, boy? Alone, alone, I should say, for youth is the time of loneliness and independence, Gene.

EUGENE

And of poetry, Major?

MAJOR

Yes, Gene: of poetry. Beauty has not died. Keats and Shelley, you know.

EUGENE

Yes, Major. They were well-known dealers in paint. What about them?

MAJOR

Why, they were young, Eugene—deathlessly young, you know.

EUGENE

Major, they were old as hell. All of the poetry has been written by old men who grew young backward.

MAJOR

Almost fiercely

No, by youth, youth—fierce beautiful youth. Give it to me again.

ACT TWO

EUGENE

Rushing like a wave beyond his mockery

Youth, youth! The old man's dream, the old man's lie! Youth with its courage and independence! Major, no more of this antique cant. Youth! From such as us are armies made, where cowardice is the slave of ridicule and fear. Youth, youth! That degrading and destructive brotherhood which can do nothing alone, and which must go forever pooled against identities; that emptiness so complete as not to contain even the seed of its own destruction; that boredom so entire that nothing may challenge its life; that banal communism of pawing hands and weaving bodies, which must feed, drink, love, think, and die together: which cries for freedom and makes the group; which is fearful, huddled, kept. Youth, the inaugurator of idiot and cowardly rebellions, which does not understand, but can only deny. It has no beautiful superstitions; it has only mean ones and ugly ones; it is the creator of terms of odium for its grandfather, and it has one triumphant formula, which courses its skull like a poisonous rat. "We have gotten beyond all that." And it uses it when it has done nothing but change its shirt. Youth! Give you your youth! Give me, my God, my age, my age—a tiny kernel of fruition. Youth! Of all mean lies this is the lowest; of all great trickeries the most believed.

MAJOR

Almost fiercely

It is not true! I say, it is not true, Eugene.

EUGENE

Major, there is only one thing that exceeds the stupidity of young men: that is the stupidity of old men. By God, I am filled with sudden woe because all the people in the world have not been born middle-aged.

> *He goes out and passes under the window.*
> *The* GENERAL *enters, groomed and washed.*

MAJOR

> *Casting suddenly his mask aside; speaking in an altered quiet voice*

When shall a man be mad?

GENERAL

As is Prince Hamlet?

MAJOR

Yes.

GENERAL

When sanity is destruction and a curse; when the eye shall pierce too far.

MAJOR

When the secret thing that all men know is spoken; when men grow false and follow Truth; when our great Falsehood—

GENERAL

That is our crown—

MAJOR

Shall be a butt for mockery. We are loyal to the destiny of ruin and death; that is the secret thing that all men know,

that I have seen in all men's eyes. In that is our only brotherhood. When the manner goes, then are we naked—
> *Bugles are blown faintly on the road.*

GENERAL

Oh, blind and bitter ship, sail home!

MAJOR

> *Lighting a cigar*

What did you say?

GENERAL

It was very bad to lose.

MAJOR

> *Puffing at his cigar*

History will justify us.

GENERAL

That was ever the maiden's prayer, so to speak.

MAJOR

The ignorant and unenlightened will say, of course, that
the war was fought on the issue of slavery.

GENERAL

You would find me on the side of the ignorant and unenlightened.

MAJOR

Slavery!

GENERAL

Nothing else! The institution of human slavery. I was fight-
ing to preserve it, because I believed in it with all my heart.
So did you, I think. So did we all.

MAJOR

Stammering

But, see here—state's rights, you know—besides—

Impatiently

Good heavens!—we must have a moral issue.

GENERAL

Impatiently

Oh, nonsense! If you begin on moral issues, you will force me to begin on the Ten Commandments. Let us avoid that, by all means.

MAJOR

But slaves—our property, you see. Puts us in a bad light, you know. Looks selfish.

GENERAL

Sharply

Take care—you are unarmed.

EUGENE *returns.*

MAJOR

In his former tone—high, thick, wheezing

Eugene, why did we go to war?

EUGENE

Some of us because we had lived in Georgia all our lives and wanted to see Virginia.

GENERAL

Pshaw, boy! That's no reason!

ACT TWO

Going

It is, if you live in Georgia.

GENERAL

Where are you going?

EUGENE

To make prayers to the Unknown God.

He goes out.

MAJOR

And so, for our slaves—

GENERAL

Sharply

For an institution; for a method of life that seems to me to
have something of the divinely ordained about it. I have
offered three lives in a war, and surrendered one! Do you
think it was for a few blacks only, who will always stay
with me anyway? No, no—there was more than that. One
God, few masters, many men. And so shall we see the happy
land of Canaan.

They rise.

MAJOR

Confidentially

By the way—

GENERAL

Yes?

MAJOR

I hesitate to speak at this time—you will tell me if it is any
embarrassment?

GENERAL

Yes, what is it?

MAJOR

I am temporarily a bit hard pressed—

GENERAL

Quickly

Of course, you will let me help you.

MAJOR

Now, you must tell me if it is inconvenient.

GENERAL

Not a bit, I assure you. How much do you need, Major?

MAJOR

Pondering

I thought, perhaps—shall we say one hundred and fifty?

GENERAL

Oh, by all means.

He begins to fumble in his pockets one by one.
Jovially

By the way, Major, will you have it in our native currency, or in the coin of the enemy?

MAJOR

Winking

I think I shall waive patriotic considerations for the moment.

GENERAL

In vexation

Pshaw! I'm out of ready currency myself, at the moment!

[124]

ACT TWO

MAJOR

Hastily

Oh, please say no more. I quite understand! Besides it doesn't matter.

GENERAL

However, I shall just give you a check for the amount.

MAJOR

By all means. I much prefer a check.

GENERAL

Sitting at his desk

"Pay to the order of Major Robert Patton, the sum of one hundred and fifty dollars."

MAJOR

Scribbling on a pad

I must give you my I.O.U.

GENERAL

Not at all necessary. Word's as good as your bond, Major!

MAJOR

Oh, yes, but I will. You must really learn to be more businesslike in these affairs, General—even when your friends are concerned—"I shall pay to the order of William Ramsay the sum of one hundred and fifty dollars—

He ponders a moment and concludes

just as soon as I am able"—there's my name.

GENERAL

Tendering the check

Here you are, Major.

[125]

MAJOR

Thanks very much. By the way, hadn't you better date it?

GENERAL

Of course—This is———?

MAJOR

The eighteenth.

GENERAL

Wetting a pen, pausing suddenly in vexation

How stupid of me!

MAJOR

What is it?

GENERAL

I have just remembered my account is overdrawn. I received notice only the other day.

MAJOR

It's quite all right.

GENERAL

However, I shall simply give you the check, and you may fill in the date as soon as I make a deposit.

MAJOR

Entirely satisfied

The very thing.

Gratefully

You have helped me out of a real difficulty, General.

GENERAL

Modestly

Oh, it's nothing—a trifle. Please don't mention it.

ACT TWO

PORTER, *still flensing his terrible hand, still nodding and winking with a cocky little birdlike movement, appears at the door and knocks.*

MAJOR

Ah, there you are, Porter!

PORTER

With a nod and a wink
Big as life, Major.

MAJOR

To GENERAL
You know Porter, eh?

GENERAL

Coldly
I know Porter.
EUGENE *enters by window.*

MAJOR

Porter has done well—he has gone into the lumber business. Very good prices for timber, I believe. Twenty-five and fifty cents an acre, I'm told.

EUGENE

What! For trees! Why, this is liberal.

MAJOR

Going to sell mine—no use for it. Taxes, you know, thought you'd like to talk with him.

GENERAL

Yes, certainly. But not today.

[127]

PORTER

With a nod and a wink

Any time, General. One day's as good as t'other with me.

GENERAL

I am just back from a war, you know! There has been a war, Porter.

PORTER

With a swift contortion of his face

Yes, General.

EUGENE

Quietly

We are sorry about your boy, Porter.

A pause

GENERAL

Calmly, coldly

Ah, yes. I had forgotten!

PORTER

In a low voice

H'it don't matter.

Fiercely

He was a fool—a fool!

GENERAL

Going

Another day, Porter. Eugene, shake hands with the gentleman.

ACT TWO

EUGENE

Turning away quickly

Ah, General!

GENERAL

Comrades, you know—investors of the future. Besides, I have taken my gloves off.

EUGENE

You, General and Porter are true comrades.

GENERAL

Coldly

I do not understand.

He goes out with the MAJOR.

PORTER *is devouring the room, and all its fittings with ravenous eyes, flensing his scorbutic hand as he gazes, and smiling ever a queer, meditative, calculating smile.*

EUGENE

In a low harsh tone

A fine house, eh, Porter?

PORTER'S *only answer is a birdlike nod and wink.*

Advancing on the man slowly

It needs paint! It needs a great many things—but it's a good house yet, eh, Porter?

PORTER

With another nod and wink, flensing his hand

Sound as the day it was built, Mister Gene.

[129]

EUGENE

They built good houses in those times, Porter.

PORTER *nods and winks.*

But it's not for sale. What a pity we're damned together, Porter. What a pity.

> PORTER *laughs suddenly—a shrill, hard, ratty treble, and plunges his scaly hand into one pocket. When he withdraws it, it is filled with shining silver coins. He jingles them softly in his hand. He goes, backing out slowly, devouring the walls, the floors, the ceilings with the hot red eyes, and flensing the back of his terrible hand. And ever as he goes he touches the objects of the room with a stubby finger, now feeling with pleasure the smooth grain of the table, now drawing his hand gently across the back of a chair, now rapping gently and knowingly against the wood of the column.* TOD *comes upon him swiftly from the porch and he goes with haste.* EUGENE *has followed every movement with dull, black eyes which blaze with hidden fire. He is quite still after the man has gone; thin bugle notes are sounded from the road.* MARGARET *enters. He does not notice her.*

MARGARET

In a whisper

Eugene! My dear, my dear—what is it?

EUGENE

I have lost something in the sun. I cannot find it—there is no moon.

> *A long pause*

ACT TWO

MARGARET

In a low voice

I understand, but you will never find it—you have killed it in the dark.

He bends his head slowly. A pause

It is dead, dead.

EUGENE

Lady, I have grown tired of seeking shadows.

MARGARET

In an almost inaudible voice

You need not love, dear. But—be true! Be true!

EUGENE

To what, lady?

MARGARET

To the past.

EUGENE

That is the loyalty of a ghost. We are not dead together.

MARGARET

In open entreaty

You are not yourself.

EUGENE

No? Then who am I?

MARGARET

Your father's son, I hope.

EUGENE

I cannot go on with Mass; it has become a mummery.

MARGARET

In a frightened voice

Eugene!

EUGENE

Oh, God, but I am weary for an ancient earth.

MARGARET

Quietly

I do not understand.

EUGENE

No. For I have seen what I have no right to remember.

MARGARET

You are mad.

EUGENE

I have opened a window on the world. There is no return.
Oh, God, but I am weary of old dreams!

A pause

MARGARET

*In a low voice, alive for the first time with repulsion
and dislike*

You—you turncoat!

*He flinches, as if he has received a blow in the face;
then he bends his head slowly, calmly.*

EUGENE

Even so!

MARGARET

*Turns her small drugged face in silent passion. En-
treatingly. Dropping her mask suddenly*

Come back! I have always known. Come back! I know!
I know! I know. Dear, we have died together.

EUGENE

Margaret, while you were yet alive—
Abruptly
I cannot rescue smoke from ashes.
Quietly, gently
Margaret, I see you in the glimmering dusk; the spectral
world is dim beyond you. I stand upon the solid shores of
earth; I may not come to where you are; there is mist and
void and darkness.

MARGARET

It is death! death! Because my life is dying in the dust with-
out you.
She moves nearer.
Oh, little God, I love you. Put your hand upon me—let me
know that you are there. Wound me with your language.
She opens her breast for him.
Defile me with your touch, as you did before; soil me, stain
me. But tell me you believe I live again.
Silence save for the merciless drop of water

EUGENE

Margaret, the horsemen on the road have gone by forever.

MARGARET

It is not too late; we may yet be saved!
A pause
You loved me once.

[133]

In a tone of fear and wonder
—or did it happen?

EUGENE

Don't you remember, ghost. Before you died—

MARGARET

Whispering
Some day—some day—

EUGENE

Some day. Who knows? The roads lead back if we go far enough.

MARGARET

Going
Some day—please waken me.

EUGENE

Starting
Margaret! You believe that!

MARGARET

With all my heart.
A pause

EUGENE

Quietly
Then, which of us is the ghost? Perhaps we live when we believe, we dream. I no longer doubt the reality of my life. I no longer expect awakening. Perhaps it is I who have died.
The MAJOR *and the* GENERAL *enter the room.*

MAJOR

My dear, we must be going. Are you quite ready?

ACT TWO

MARGARET

Yes, Father. I am quite ready.

The GENERAL *gives her a searching glance.*

GENERAL

You must come over again, soon, my dear.

MARGARET

I shall always be loyal, General.

GENERAL

God bless you for that, my dear.

EUGENE

It is not enough, but it will serve until a better time.

GENERAL

I pray a better time will have as much. Good-by, my dear.

He kisses her.

MAJOR

Come, Margaret. The catalogs are ready to be mailed.

The MAJOR *and* MARGARET *go.*

Bugles are sounded faintly on the road.

GENERAL

It is necessary that I be left quite alone for an hour. There is a great deal to be done—letters to be answered, and so on. I shall want you here, when our people assemble. You might make yourself more presentable, you know. Appearances are very important, remember.

EUGENE

Bowing

You shall be obeyed in all things, General. Shall I wear a sword?

GENERAL

It would be more to the point, I think, if you wore a clean shirt and a collar. No nonsense, remember.

EUGENE

Yes.

He advances a step; in a low tone earnestly

When you need me, you will call.

GENERAL

I will call.

A pause

You have been a good soldier; you mocked, but you were honest. I shall not forget.

EUGENE

You owe me nothing. We must do penance for the sin of breathing; and I've never earned a hair shirt.

He goes out.

The GENERAL *seats himself at his desk, and busies himself with letters. His manner is that of a man who returns to familiar things, and who accepts them quickly as if the period of his absence were already forgotten. He begins to write. He picks up a pen from the desk and dips it absently in the ink well which he finds dry. He strikes a small bell on the*

*table. There is no answer. He throws the pen down
with a gesture of vexation, and calls sharply.*

GENERAL

Bynum!

There is no answer. In a moment he calls again.

Bynum!

*Still no answer. Finally he calls several names in
succession.*

Bynum! . . . Jones! . . . Sam!

There is no answer and the GENERAL *rises impatiently
and angrily from his chair and strides to the corner
of the room where the bell cord hangs. He pulls the
cord sharply and violently. There is absolute silence
for a moment; then in a far corner of the house there
is a harsh jangling of aged and rusty bells.* GENERAL
RAMSAY *starts as if he has been stung; his hand is
withdrawn swiftly from the cord; he looks keenly
and searchingly around him for the first time. With
an expression of growing disbelief and horror the*
GENERAL *notes the evidence of doom and desolation
which surround him at every point—which have
touched his room, and his house, and his life; which
stare at him with fanged malevolence. And a sound,
which we have heard before, a displeasing sound,
and which has disturbed him vaguely, begins to hammer softly at the portals of his consciousness: the
sounds of the single large drop of water, which
somewhere forms, swells, develops, and falls with*

[137]

unvarying punctual monotony. GENERAL RAMSAY
walks slowly once around the borders of his room,
peering intently but fruitlessly at wall and ceiling.
He returns to the bell cord, and stretches forth his
hand again to grasp it, drawing it back again hesi-
tantly, as if afraid to face the issue. Finally he thrusts
his hand forth boldly and gives a swift, sharp tug.
The frayed and rotted cord parts in its center and
under his grasp. In the distance the bells fall to the
floor with a harsh and rusty jangle.

Somewhere in the house, a door is opened slowly,
and is closed again. Somewhere there is a stealthy
pad of feet, and in a moment the Negro, TOD, *has*
entered the room.

GENERAL

I called and no one answered! Where are my people?
The black's old head sinks slowly to his breast.
EUGENE *enters. His somber eyes are lit with flame.*

EUGENE

You have no people, General.

GENERAL

In a low tone, hoarsely
What are you saying, Eugene?

EUGENE

They have been gone a week—they left when the news
came.

ACT TWO

GENERAL

Low and hoarse

You knew, you knew, Eugene.

EUGENE

Quietly

Yes, General. The rivers are flowing backward.

> *The* GENERAL *lifts his arms with a gesture of supreme despair. Silence, save for the slow punctual falling of the merciless drop of water. Thin bugle notes, elfin, faint, remote, upon the road.*

CURTAIN

Act Two
Part Two

Time: *Toward sundown of a day in June, 1865.*

Scene: *The curtain rises on an empty room, stripped of its ornaments, save for a few articles stained and stricken as with marks of pestilence. A large deep chair is placed beside a table near the opened window; a red and smoky sun is going down beyond the spectral forests, and in the shaggy grasses of the lawn about the place, a million little creatures of the night have come to life in sound.*

Far off, a bugle blows; there is a muffled tattoo on small drums; a cannon is discharged. There are commands in staccato speech.

The door to the left is opened. The negro TOD *comes in, bearing gently and softly and lightly in his great arms the figure of the* GENERAL. *He carries him to the big chair by the window, and deposits him with tenderness and care.*

Behind the white luxuriousness of hair and beard, the phantom of a man looks on the world from deep fierce eyes, sunk, in a ruined noble head. His face is sharp and beaked like that of a great fierce bird.

GENERAL

The rug, Tod.

> TOD *goes out and returns immediately with a heavy blanket which he lays across the* GENERAL'S *knees and wraps softly under his feet.*

That is a bloody sun which sets tonight, but I would look at it once more.

> EUGENE *enters in his parade uniform. Booming of a great bell in the wind*

What is the time, Eugene?

EUGENE

It is six o'clock and through the world, excepting other longitudes, the sons of common men are coming from their work.

GENERAL

You seem excited, son. The true revolutionary spirit. Never quite happy until things begin to fall. Now, if Samson were only here to pull us down—

EUGENE

We shall escape, General, in spite of you.

> *Imperceptibly it has grown darker.*

GENERAL

> *Sharply*

Light, Tod. More light!

EUGENE

> *From the darkness*

No General. Not more light—more warmth! Men do not die of darkness, but of cold.

TOD *brings a lamp and puts it on the table.*

GENERAL

And so you think you may escape, Captain. I tell you, boy, the brand is on you; the steel has sunken deep into your soul. We are of few years and many woes. For us there is only the doom that comes unseen; for us there is no victory —there is only valiance. We are all damned together.

EUGENE

Yes, General. We are all damned together, but I must insist on my inalienable right to seek out my own particular hell.

GENERAL

And where does the pilgrim go?

EUGENE

Beyond the gates where men are; and down to the sea perhaps; and up the steepled hill to God.

GENERAL

Why, come—this is knighthood with a vengeance. He goes out with a hole in one pocket, and brimstone in the other.

EUGENE

Thank you. It's a true balance.

GENERAL

And if he's wise, he'll ride a donkey—a horse would never understand him.

EUGENE

Again, I thank you. My ears are too long to care for grace.

GENERAL

For you, my son, there is no escape. You will come back and dig the ruins.

> *A knocking at the door;* PORTER, *with his birdlike nod and wink, stands at the threshold, flensing the back of his terrible hand.*
> *Sharply*

Who is it?

EUGENE

> *In a low voice*

It is Porter.

GENERAL

> *Grimly, in a low voice*

A vulture looks best in the dark.

EUGENE

> *Going to the door*

Yes, Porter?

PORTER

> *With a nod and a wink*

Evenin'.

GENERAL

> *Genially*

Come in, Porter. I am dying. Give the gentleman a chair, Eugene.

ACT TWO

PORTER *is seated at the table, in half-darkness, opposite the* GENERAL.

PORTER
Awkwardly, uneasily
I was right sorry to hear, Mister Ramsay—

GENERAL
Laughing good humoredly
Sorry! Pshaw! Will you listen to the man? Sorry for what? Come, man. It's not every day that you can see a gentleman die.

PORTER
Yes, sir. Now, about the timber of your'n—

GENERAL
Ah, yes, the timber. Tell me, Porter—are there enough trees in my forests to timber me a coffin?

PORTER
With his birdlike nod and wink
Enough for us all, I reckon, Mister Ramsay.

GENERAL
Enough for us all. For you, too, Porter?

PORTER
For me, too.

GENERAL
Ah, that is strange. So we'll be housed in the same wood at the end—we two?

[145]

PORTER

Flensing his hand and gazing around at the walls of the room with a queer meditative smile

Yes, Mister Ramsay, I reckon we will be. *Housed* in the same wood at the end.

EUGENE

Harshly

You are quite mistaken, Porter.

PORTER

Flensing his hand, with a terrible, contorted smile

Yes, sir. A mighty fine house, yet, Mister Ramsay.

GENERAL

Softly, bending forward a little

The house? But we had said nothing about the house, Porter.

EUGENE

Sharply

Your business, Porter? My father is not well.

GENERAL

Waving a thin hand

Oh, come! This is unseemly! You must not hurry a guest in this fashion. Besides—an old friend of the family—Porter, you must pardon him.

PORTER

Hit's about that land o' your'n, Mister Ramsay.

EUGENE

Impatiently

But that has all been settled, Porter. My father has agreed to sell.

ACT TWO

Waving a deprecating hand

Eugene, I beg of you—You are wronging the intentions of our honored friend. I see it plainly: Porter has discovered that the land is rich in gold, or oil, or coal, or platinum or lapis lazuli—Being, like Brutus, an honorable man, he has come to inform us; to invite us to share in the profits.

PORTER

Nervously, clearing his throat

No, Mister Ramsay. Hit's the papers.

GENERAL

The papers! Ah, yes. There would be papers, wouldn't there?

EUGENE

Tomorrow, Porter. My father is not well tonight.

GENERAL

No, no! He comes in good season—better than you know. You have the true prophetic gift, Porter.

EUGENE

In a low voice

What do you mean, General?

PORTER

With an intent smile, staring at the GENERAL

Yes, Mister Ramsay.

GENERAL

Some birds will hover, waiting for us—Well, to our business then.

[147]

PORTER *draws a creased and folded paper from his pocket, and smooths it carefully with his blunt hands, on his knees.*

GENERAL

The papers! No play should be without them!

PORTER

Hit needs yore name.

GENERAL

To Eugene, with triumph
Do you hear?

PORTER

—To do hit legal.

GENERAL

Taking the paper
By all means, let it be done legal.
Reading carelessly
"Party of the first . . . party of the second . . ." oh, yes. There always are, aren't there? H'm. Yes. Perfectly regular, I am sure.
Reading
"And further, it is understood that the boundaries of the said tract shall be defined—"

EUGENE

Quickly
Father—tomorrow!

[148]

GENERAL

No, but I will!

Reading

"On the north, three miles along Ravel's Creek, between old Mill and Potter's Bridge; thence southwest a distance of five and three-eighths miles to the Painted Rock, along the near or eastern border of Hominy Road—"

Pushing the paper away. With a great cry

Oh, my kingdom, my kingdom!

PORTER

Flensing his hand

—To do hit legal.

EUGENE

Harshly

Be silent, Porter.

GENERAL

Reading further

—"And moreover it is agreed that, beginning on the near, or south side of Fairview Pike, the land extending east from the Painted Rock to the junction of the Fairview Pike, with the Burnsville Road, three-fifths of a mile, and ascending southward a quarter of a mile to the summit of Skyland hill . . ."

EUGENE

Desperately

Father!

GENERAL

Implacably

". . . and including upon its premises certain buildings, as quarters for servants, spring houses, stables, and the residences of sixteen rooms at its summit, known as—"

EUGENE

General! The House, the House! My God, you never told me that.

GENERAL

Sternly

Give me the pen, Eugene.

EUGENE

General—the House! You can't.

GENERAL

Give me the pen, Eugene.

A pause

PORTER

Funny, mebbe, 'bout all this. But hit's got to be. Hit's Progress!

GENERAL

Waving a transparent hand gently

And now the man has learned another word. It is, of course, a very fine word. Not only the world gets better, but all the people in it. In its essence it is the cult of pity for one's grandfather.

In the same tone as before; inflexible, unyielding

The pen, the pen, Eugene. Give me the pen.

EUGENE

Desperately, as before

General, the House! But why?

[150]

GENERAL

It must go on, Eugene.

EUGENE

Turning toward PORTER *with a puzzled futile gesture
of the hands*

To this? To this? Go on to this?

GENERAL

Here is my only hope of permanence. By God, it shall continue; under filthy and unspeakable hands it shall continue if it must. But it shall continue. Go your ways, boys. Go your ways. Our truce is almost done. Eugene, I say it shall continue!

EUGENE

In a voice without intonation

Rebel! Rebel! You have not known me for my ancient loyalty; and I believe in endings, nothing more.

GENERAL

The pen.

EUGENE *wets a pen and gives it to the* GENERAL.

EUGENE

Yes, General.

GENERAL

Scrawling laboriously

In good season, Porter. In very good season. Yet, how easily it is done. And thus I sign my abdictation; your rights as heir apparent. Where is your kingdom now, my boy?

EUGENE

Coldly, triumphantly

Throughout the whole wide world. I have lost a kingdom, and gained an empire. The bargain is good.

GENERAL

Inheritor of smoke and dreams! We are all damned together!

PORTER

Giving the paper to EUGENE

Now you sign your'n.

EUGENE

And why, Porter?

PORTER

To do hit legal—witness hit.

EUGENE

Signing

It is witnessed, Porter.

PORTER *refolds the paper carefully, puts it in his purse, and rises.*

PORTER

Yore money will be in the bank tomorrow, Mister Ramsay.

GENERAL

Why, that is splendid, Porter.

PORTER

Flensing his hand

I ain't so fine as some folks, mebbe, but I pay up prompt.

ACT TWO

GENERAL

Porter, you have all the successful virtues and none of the gentlemanly ones. You were small today; you will be great tomorrow.

PORTER

Grinning

"Blessed are the meek, for they shall inherit the earth."

GENERAL

They always did—six feet of it.

PORTER

Slowly

Next time I see yo—

GENERAL

Slowly

Next time? Then you had not heard, Porter?

PORTER

Puzzled

No, sir.

GENERAL

I am going away—on a journey.

EUGENE

Desperately

Father—don't.

A pause

PORTER

Flensing his hand, his face contorted suddenly with terrible malevolence

You're an old man.

EUGENE

With a fierce movement toward the man

By God, you—

GENERAL

Sharply

Stop!

PORTER

With a cry high in his throat

I've paid ye now! I've paid ye for hit all.

EUGENE

You had better go, I think.

PORTER

In a low voice, suddenly

He was a fool! A fool!

A slight pause

They're all damned fools at twenty.

Muttering, moving backward slowly

I'll be goin'.

GENERAL

What! You must go so soon! But stay—stay for a little as my guest, Porter. They are going to light some candles presently.

PORTER

Shortly

Good night to both of ye!

GENERAL

With a resigned manner

Oh well, if you must. Give the gentleman your hand, Eugene.

EUGENE

Turning away with a desperate movement

General—don't.

GENERAL

Softly

"And we hold that all men are, or ought to be—"

EUGENE

In God's name, General!

GENERAL

Sharply

Captain! I command!

EUGENE

Quietly

You are quite right. There is yet a truce. Here is my hand, Porter.

He gives it to him.

GENERAL

Gently

How touching! One of your brothers! Tell the gentleman you are very glad he called, Eugene.

[155]

EUGENE

Steadily

I am very glad you called, Porter.

GENERAL

Now show him to the door.

> EUGENE *goes to the door with* PORTER *who turns, still with his contorted smile, and pauses for a moment.*

EUGENE

In a low voice

Remember, Porter, that for you, too, there can be no victory. There is an ending for us all.

PORTER

There's timber enough for us both, Mr. Ramsay.

> *He goes quickly into the darkness.*

EUGENE

Returning

I have heard that it takes all kinds to make a world.

GENERAL

Generally there is room for only one kind at a time. Go tell your mother to come here.

> EUGENE *goes.*
>
> *Calling*

Tod!

> *The Negro enters.*

We are delivered into the hands of the barbarians.

ACT TWO

TOD

Bending swiftly over his master, pointing to the door and darkness

Kill!

GENERAL

Not yet, my boy. We do these things too clumsily. Let us give God a chance.

TOD goes out. In a moment MRS. RAMSAY *comes in softly.*

Are you there, my dear?

MRS. RAMSAY

Yes. You sent for me?

GENERAL

Come closer, into the light.

She advances.

How young you are tonight.

MRS. RAMSAY

Hardly audible

Don't, my dear.

GENERAL

I cannot come to you as I did once. Will you kneel here at my chair, where I may look at you?

She sinks slowly on her knees before him, within the dim circle of light which the lamp gives.

So we'll go no more a-roving,
So late into the night.

[157]

MRS. RAMSAY

My life has been a pattern, but I lived it. I was always a child, and you loved me.

GENERAL

Placing his thin hands on her head

Oh, little child, I love you now, when I too have become a child!

MRS. RAMSAY

And if I had grown up, my dear?

GENERAL

I could never have loved you half so much. For I come of a foolish creed of men who must play at being mighty—for God needs laughter, and only the child in you could heal my broken pride.

MRS. RAMSAY

Oh, my king; my great, strong man, you are triumphant. And you will walk upon the stars.

GENERAL

With a grim smile

It is a good suggestion, wife. I have nothing else to walk upon.

MRS. RAMSAY

Resting her head, as a child, upon his hand

You must not go! You must not go! Oh, dearest, who will lead me if you go!

GENERAL

We have had wine and music; we must rest.

ACT TWO

MRS. RAMSAY

Ah, it has been such a little time—a little time.

With a desperate cry

My God, how is it we are old!

GENERAL

The best dreams are too short—to sleep, to sleep, I think, is best.

MRS. RAMSAY

To love is best; it is more strong than death.

GENERAL

Not love, but time.

He kisses her gently.

I shall remember you always as I saw you first, in the morning, in the light, in the sun—when you came to me from your father's house. I cannot see you for the dark—you belong to the rose and radiance. Go sleep, then until morning.

MRS. RAMSAY

Rising

I will come to you then.

GENERAL

Good night, my dear.

He kisses her and she goes.

Silence for a time. A wind about the house far off; the beating of great wings upon the air

Calling

Eugene!

[159]

EUGENE *enters.*

I tell you now that there can be no victory. There is only valiance.

EUGENE

There is only valiance.

GENERAL

We are forever beaten; we are proud, and we are forever cast down; we are forever broken by His strength; and at last we always die.

EUGENE

Yes, General.

GENERAL

How good it is to struggle then, when there is nothing but defeat.

A pause

Go bring my sword, Eugene.

EUGENE

But now—

GENERAL

Sternly

At once.

EUGENE *goes out and returns with the General's sword, and places it across his knees. An old wind blows about the house and as it dies the slow beating of mighty wings quite near are heard.*

Listening intently, in a low voice

He comes, he comes—the ancient enemy! And in the dark, Eugene!

EUGENE

Yes, General.

GENERAL

With triumph in his voice

He did not dare to come by day!

A pause. A door swings open in the house.

Come close, Eugene, and let me hold your hand.

EUGENE

Approaching

I am here.

GENERAL

I cannot see you, Gene, for it is dark. Oh, boy—our eagles
are flown away, and I am dust. What have I left you for
your faith?

EUGENE

A song, for all valiant men.

GENERAL

Then say the word, Eugene.

EUGENE

Valiance.

GENERAL

So be it now, he comes.

*Wind blows hard against the house. The window is
swung open in the dark. Leaning forward in his chair*

And are you there?

EUGENE

What is it, Father?

GENERAL

Someone has come, and stands there in the darkness by the window. Do you see, Eugene?

EUGENE

I do not see, General.

GENERAL

And do you believe that he is there?
A pause

EUGENE

Quietly

I believe that he is there.

GENERAL

I have believed for all my days in what could not be seen—in smoke, in some perhaps; in hidden faith, and secret honor, in all the beauty and the mystery in the hearts of men; and now I fall before you like an old tree to the wind; to inherit the dark and the dust.

EUGENE

The enemy has taken much; he could not take your mighty heart. You will inherit God tonight, dear General.

GENERAL

I ask of Him who gave me ruin no more than sleep. For I am desolate and old, and have forgotten Heaven. Oh, son, the period of your truce draws to an end.

EUGENE

Quietly

I do not ask it, Father.

GENERAL

Yes, you may take the braid and buttons from your jacket when you will. Tinsel! Tinsel! You said so once.

EUGENE

Yes, General.

GENERAL

My God, but it was worth it.

He rises.

Sharply

But you are waiting in the dark, my friend. Perhaps you thought to find me unprepared. But, come—I have been waiting for you. Or did you think to find me hiding in my chair?

EUGENE

Father!

GENERAL

With a fierce cry, swinging the great sword in a gleaming arc

Come on, come on, my friend. I have met worse than you in the open field.

A pause. The GENERAL *lets his sword sink slowly to his side. In a small voice*

My God! And what is this? This is the conqueror! A wretched, blind old man with fumbling hands, who mumbles jargon in his throat, and feels his way along the table.

Very gently

A moment more, my friend; and you may lean on me, for I am strong; and we will go together.

Booming of a great bell, in the wind is heard.
Gene! Are you there, boy, in the dark?

EUGENE

I am here!

GENERAL

The time is short. The word, boy, once again.

EUGENE

Valiance!

GENERAL

Triumphantly
The manner, the manner—the bold, great manner!
Swinging the great sword feebly
And now, God be praised, who crushes me. I have died, as
I lived, with a great gesture.
He sinks slowly forward. EUGENE *catches him in his
arms.*

EUGENE

Father! Father!
Beating of great wings, loud and close

GENERAL

Through stiffening lips
Oh, boy, you have been faithful—

EUGENE

Desperately
General, in God's name—Don't! Don't!

[164]

ACT TWO

Almost inaudibly

The truce is ended! Go where they call you, Pilgrim, on the road.

> *He pitches forward in* EUGENE'S *arms.* EUGENE *lowers him gently into the chair.*

EUGENE

Yes, General! Now the truce is ended!

> *To himself with terrible conviction*

Yes—I have died.

> *Slowly, one by one, he begins to strip the buttons from his jacket.*
>
> *Beating of mighty wings far off and faint. Thin and audible laughter near at hand. The lamp is blown out.*

CURTAIN

Act Three

TIME: *After the ruinous years of Reconstruction have passed.*

SCENE: *When the curtain rises late afternoon has come, a small sun, dim and smoky red, is low above the dark trees of the forest.*

From within the house from every quarter, there is a steady din of hammering, and the sounds of boards, wrenched with a heavy rasp from their moorings in the wall.

Backward, forward, coming in with empty hands, going out again bent low under heavy burdens of old wood, an endless chain of black men, but this time in stained and dirty clothes, are entering and leaving the house.

Within the room two white men, carpenters, are beating old boards from the wall and floor with heavy hammers.

FIRST CARPENTER

Well, sir, she took hold of that thing and she give it one look an' she said, "Gre-ee-at God, Almighty."

SECOND CARPENTER

Mister, yore wife'll whup you, if she knows whar you're spendin' yore spare time. A feller over on Hominy Creek got to goin' with a gal an' he bigged her. Now he spends all his time hidin' out in the woods a-munchin' nuts like a goddam squirrel.

FIRST CARPENTER

What fer?

SECOND CARPENTER

He cain't go home. He tried to once an' his old woman met him at the door with a shot gun. She got him in the seat o' the pants just as he was goin' out o' the gate.

FIRST CARPENTER

Laughing coarsely

God Almighty! I reckon he ain't sat down yet.

SECOND CARPENTER

Last I heard tell of him he was still in the woods, apickin' buckshot out with a screw driver.

They laugh with coarse big hilarity, slapping their thighs.

FIRST CARPENTER

Ole man's wust I ever seen. He'd save skin off'n a sausage. What's he want with these ole boards.

SECOND CARPENTER

Good timber heah yet.

EUGENE *comes in, neatly clothed and weary of the road.*

[168]

ACT THREE

FIRST CARPENTER

Roughly

Did ye finish at the mill?

EUGENE

Yes.

EUGENE *retires to a corner, starts working.*

SECOND CARPENTER

The old man'll hire any tramp that comes along. Gits 'em for next to nothin'. Don't like workin' with 'em, neither. Lazy an' shif'less.

FIRST CARPENTER

This 'un worked hard today. No foolin'.

SECOND CARPENTER

Ole man was watching.

PORTER *comes in flensing his hand. He has been drinking. They become studiously busy.*

PORTER

Got yore pay, didn't ye?

FIRST CARPENTER

Yes, sir.

PORTER

Allus got it prompt, ain't ye?

FIRST CARPENTER

Yes, sir.

PORTER

Tend to yore damn business.

SECOND CARPENTER

Muttering

Ain't hired to wo'k with a tramp.

PORTER

Go t'hell.

MARGARET *enters wearing a hat.*

MARGARET

To CARPENTER

You do not mind if I look around, do you?

FIRST CARPENTER

No, ma'am.

They regard her curiously, and whisper among themselves and then go out.

MARGARET

How do you do, Mr. Porter.

PORTER

Flensing his hand

Miss Patton, ain't hit?

MARGARET

Yes.

PORTER

Didn't know ye with yore hat on.

MARGARET

Pleasantly

No? Shall I take it off, Mr. Porter?

[170]

ACT THREE

PORTER

Pointing with a nod and a wink to where EUGENE
bends low in a corner, his back to them

New hand. He'll show ye 'round. Funny feller. Like funny
fellers, don't ye?

PORTER *goes out.*

MARGARET

You are a new man, aren't you?

EUGENE

Yes, lady.

MARGARET

A stranger here?

EUGENE

Yes, lady.

MARGARET

There are a great many new people here, I believe.

EUGENE

Yes, lady. I believe so.
A pause

MARGARET

Do you always talk to people with your back turned?

EUGENE

Yes, lady. Whenever I can.

MARGARET

It is becoming quite dark, and I cannot see you very well.
Will you turn around?

[171]

EUGENE

In a low voice

Yes, lady.

He faces her slowly, and they look at each other for a long level moment.

MARGARET

In a low voice

You see, I was right. It is becoming quite dark.

EUGENE

Yes, lady.

MARGARET

And you do not see me very well, do you.

EUGENE

Not very well.

MARGARET

But a little—you see me a little?

EUGENE

I see your eyes, lady—I could see them very well even if I were far off.

MARGARET

And in the dark?

EUGENE

Yes. In the dark.

MARGARET

And in the light you could not tell that I have grown old?

EUGENE

No, lady. In this light I could not tell that you were anything but young, and deathless, and forever lovely.

MARGARET

What a beautiful thing is darkness, then.

EUGENE

Yes, lady. More true than dawn; more hopeful than the sun.

MARGARET

And on what road did you learn that?

EUGENE

There are no answers, lady; there are no questions.

MARGARET

And is that all?

EUGENE

That is all. There is only the distance and all the pain.

MARGARET

It was for that you sought the world!

EUGENE

It was for that. The ends of the earth are met in darkness—
I shall not go beyond it.

MARGARET

    With a sudden cry

My God, my God, Eugene—but they have hurt you!

EUGENE

    With a touch of mockery

Have you not heard? The brothers kill each other in the
dark.

MARGARET

You will not go again.

EUGENE

I shall not go again, ghost. Put your hands upon me in the dark—for I am desolate and sick. Your touch may heal me.

MARGARET

Eugene! Eugene!
> *He kisses her.*

EUGENE

Go away, go away, my ghost. I will come when my work is over.

MARGARET

> *Going*

I shall heal you and make you well, Eugene.

EUGENE

Go away, little ghost, go away.
> *She goes.*
> *A whistle is blown. The* CARPENTERS, *bearing their kits of tools, go through the room toward the entrance.*

FIRST CARPENTER

> *Sharply*

What ye hangin' round fer? Heah the whistle?

EUGENE

Yes, centurion. I am going.

FIRST CARPENTER

> *Angrily*

What'd you call me?

EUGENE

Je voudrai faire le pipi.

SECOND CARPENTER

Leave him alone. You can't expect no different from a tramp.

To EUGENE, *roughly*

Go 'long now an' don't go callin' decent people names.

EUGENE

Be quiet, Carpenter. I can see plainly that you have ancestors.

SECOND CARPENTER

Furiously, moving forward

Did ye hear that, hey?

PORTER

Entering, flensing his hand

Go 'long, go 'long! Ye heard the whistle.

FIRST CARPENTER

Ain't paid t'be insulted by—

PORTER

Get out.

They go. In the gathering dusk the blacks tramp heavily out in a solid and implacable wedge.

EUGENE

And the day is done for me as well, my good kind master?

PORTER

Fer you! Why, ye must learn tonight how houses are torn down.

[175]

EUGENE

And you will teach me, master?

PORTER

I'll teach ye sure enough—you've never handled tools 'fore this?

EUGENE

No.

>*The gentle voices and the music are heard, far off.*

And do you hear the music in the house, good master?

PORTER

>*Grimly*

I can tell the best joke now, my son.

EUGENE

You do not hear? Then the mark is not upon you yet, good master.

PORTER

>*Approaching*

You sure you ain't never handled tools before, have ye?

EUGENE

>*Using the hammer clumsily*

No.

PORTER

>*With a contorted smile, flensing his hand*

Never learned when you growed, I reckon.

EUGENE

No.

[176]

ACT THREE

PORTER

I'll show ye how hit's done. Give me the hammer.

EUGENE *gives it to him.*

Hold hit like this—d'ye see?

EUGENE

Nodding, taking the hammer again

Yes.

PORTER

With his contorted smile

Now, I reckon we'll have to have somethin' to use hit on, won't we?

EUGENE

Yes.

PORTER

Coming closer

Mebbe you'd better pick somethin' out—an' I'll show ye how it's done.

EUGENE

I think you had better pick it out.

PORTER *seats himself in the General's chair.*

Quickly

You had better sit here, hadn't you?

He indicates another chair.

PORTER

Flensing his hand, grinning

What fer?

EUGENE

It's an old chair—this one is better for you.

PORTER

Reflectively, striking the arm of the chair

An old chair? Pshaw! Hit's good as th' day hit was made.

As if struck by a sudden idea

Look heah! I'll show ye how good hit is.

He gets up quickly.

Whar's the hammer?

EUGENE

Here it is.

He gives it to him.

PORTER

Ye hold, but like this—

He indicates.

—an ye hit it like this.

He deals a savage blow which demolishes one arm of the chair.

EUGENE

Hoarsely

You mustn't do that, do you hear?

PORTER

With a smile of malevolent innocence
Flensing his terrible hand

What fer? Hit's only an' ole chair. You were right about hit. Hit ain't as good as I thought hit was.

Laughing shrilly

[178]

Looky thar!

> *He deals another savage and demolishing blow.*

EUGENE

> *Reeling on his feet*

No, no! You mustn't do that!

PORTER

> *Becoming quiet*

What's that? Mustn't do hit?

> *As if comprehending suddenly*

Oh, I see! Ye don't want me to smash hit up! Ye want me to keep hit fer myself.

> *He seats himself.*

Why you're all right, *you* bastard! A smart fellow! I'll jest do that. Hit jest fits me, don't hit?

EUGENE

> *In a low voice*

Yes. It fits you very well, master.

PORTER

The ole man hisse'f, eh.

> *Rising*

Now, you do hit. I'll jest look on. This table—mebbe—er the mantel—see how easy hit is.

> *He strikes the mantel with the hammer.*

You try hit now.

> *He gives* EUGENE *the hammer.*

EUGENE

Yes, upon your dirty skull, my good master.

PORTER

In a sudden shrill voice

All right, out thar! Help!

EUGENE *hurls himself upon the man and throttles him.
The* CARPENTERS *run in, and overcome him.*

Gasping

Throw the bastard out.

EUGENE

But remember that there are endings for us both, good
master.

FIRST CARPENTER

No, you don't, you damn tramp!

SECOND CARPENTER

Come along now.

EUGENE *is led out. The* CARPENTERS *return.*

PORTER

Flensing his terrible hand

See that he gits his pay. Git along, thar, now. An' don't
fergit to clean up the mess first thing tomorrow. He tried
to smash things up.

PORTER *follows* CARPENTERS *out.*

MARGARET'S VOICE

Far up in the house

Eugene!

EUGENE

Returns. He can be seen through the front door

[180]

where he has appeared on the porch, leaning wearily
against the column.

Oh, I am coming, ghost.

MARGARET'S VOICE

Softly

Then come, oh, come, Eugene.

EUGENE

With one hand on the column

I am a part of all that I have touched.

MARGARET'S VOICE

Whispering

Then come, Eugene.

The sun, streaked with red filaments of smoke, gives
a dim and fading light to the interior of the house.

EUGENE

Tracing the wording of the ancient scroll

Nil Separabit.

With a cry

Oh, my fathers were valiant men!

He wraps his gaunt arms fiercely round the column.
There is a convulsive movement of his ruined frame,
and he wrenches the column from its rotted base as
he strains it to his breast. It falls upon him slowly,
and he is borne to the earth, and lies at length athwart
the shallow steps, his gaunt face turned toward the
setting sun.

Far off within the house there is a mighty thrill, a

[181]

great, growing vibration, which trembles through the walls. A heavy timber is heard to bend and buckle. PORTER *and the* CARPENTERS *run in past* EUGENE'S *prostrate form on the steps, across the porch and into the room.*

EUGENE *calls faintly from where he lies beneath the fallen column.*

Tod! Tod! Oh, I have failed! Tod! Here was a house. It was by you begun; by you it must be ended. Tod! Tod!

From somewhere inside the house the Negro, TOD *leaps like a cat into the room, and thrusts his great body toward the outer door.*

The others spring upon him, and he throws them back. PORTER *rushes upon the Negro with a drawn knife and stabs him repeatedly in the breast.*

The Negro, with a smile of savage triumph, which reveals his yellow fangs, makes no resistance, but when the man is done, sinks slowly forward upon him, and breaks him in his mighty grip.

TOD *falls slowly forward upon the floor. The* CARPENTERS *attempt to rush to safety, pass* TOD'S *body, and the broken frame of* PORTER.

A timber falls slantwise across the door, and they are held.

The men are flattened to the walls in terror; they fix their eyes aloft as on some nameless and unfathomable horror which they cannot see—a tiny spurt of white dust sifts down upon their faces, their heads,

ACT THREE

*their clothes. The great vibrations within the house
lengthen to a thunder.*

PORTER, *dying, lies half against the door sill, his eyes
fixed on something which is plunging down on him
from above, his mouth twisted in its queer terrible,
contorted smile, his stubby fingers flensing, as before,
his unspeakable hand.*

THE CURTAIN DROPS QUICKLY

*There is heard immediately a terrific crash and the
sounds of heavy timbers, which buckle and settle.
There is a lesser reverberation, followed by silence,
save for the faint far ending of a waltz which dies
upon the wind; save for a merciless little drop of
water which somewhere swells, develops, and falls
at length with punctual, unvarying monotony.*

A THIN VOICE

Faint and far
Snap your fingers, gentlemen.

THE END

Set in Linotype Janson
Format by A. W. Rushmore
Manufactured by The Haddon Craftsmen
Published by HARPER & BROTHERS, *New York*